TWAYNE'S WORLD AUTHORS SERIES
A Survey of the World's Literature

Sylvia E. Bowman, Indiana University

GENERAL EDITOR

SPAIN

Gerald E. Wade, Vanderbilt University
Janet Winecoff Díaz, University of North Carolina at Chapel Hill

EDITORS

Cervantes

TWAS 329

Cervantes

Cervantes

By Manuel Durán

Yale University

TWAYNE PUBLISHERS
A DIVISION OF G. K. HALL & CO., BOSTON

Library of Congress Cataloging in Publication Data

Durán, Manuel, 1925-
Cervantes.

(Twayne's world author series, TWAS 329. Spain)
Bibliography: p. 185.
1. Cervantes Saavedra, Miguel de, 1547-1616.
PQ6337.D84   863'.3   74-7006
ISBN 0-8057-2206-8

Contents

About the Author

Manuel Durán, a native of Barcelona, Spain, studied in Spain, France, Mexico and the U.S. He holds a Ph.D. in Romance Languages and Literatures from Princeton University where he worked under Prof. Américo Castro and other distinguished teachers. He is Professor of Spanish Literature at Yale University. He has published a book on Cervantes, *La ambigüedad en el Quijote*, as well as important critical essays on Góngora, Lope de Vega, Quevedo, and the Marquis of Santillana. His *Luis de León* appeared in Twayne's World Authors Series in 1971 and has been very well received by the critics. A Guggenheim Fellow for 1964, Manuel Durán has lectured extensively on Spanish literature both in the U.S. and abroad. His articles have appeared in some of the most important magazines in Europe, the U.S., and Latin America. Manuel Durán has authored or edited 23 books and more than 100 articles and essays.

Preface

There are writers whose works do not travel well: They have to be appreciated in or near the place where they were produced, like certain types of wine. Others on the contrary seem to gain by crossing national borders. Cervantes belongs to this last group.

It is not easy to define what makes a writer truly universal. It is far easier to pinpoint why certain works are not readily accepted beyond the boundaries of the culture that helped to create them. Francisco de Quevedo and Luis de Góngora, for instance, were great writers living in Cervantes' Spain whose works have never been fully appreciated by readers from other cultures. Their Baroque poetry is impossible to translate. Even Quevedo's prose is often obscure or is based upon puns and allusions that have no meaning in other languages. Cervantes' aim was to be both clear and amusing. This is the advice he gives to himself in the Prologue to *Don Quixote:* "You have only to see that your sentences shall come out plain, in expressive, sober and well-ordered language, harmonious and gay, expressing your purpose to the best of your ability, and setting out your ideas without intricacies and obscurities. Be careful too that the reading of your story makes the melancholy laugh and the merry laugh louder; that the simpleton is not confused; that the intelligent admire your invention, the serious do not despise it, nor the prudent withhold their praise."[1]

Cervantes' style is varied and supple, never obscure. This clarity—unfashionable at the time he wrote his novels and short stories—has turned in the long run to be a great asset. As a professional writer (which means that he hoped to earn a living by writing books: He did not always succeed, but his goal was always present in his mind) he aimed for a large public. He found it with the publication of the first part of *Don Quixote* in 1605: His success was immediate and lasting, both inside and outside Spain (a pirated edition appeared in Lisbon in the same year, others were to follow in several European cities). Cervantes' language, as seen in the context of his period, is clearer than most. What does his message mean to us? Most modern readers may fall back upon two key words:

"humor" and "realism." It is much easier to define "humor"—since after all, we all know what amuses us, what makes us laugh—than "realism"—since the definition of "realism" or "reality" is a philosophical problem, one of the most arduous philosophical problems of all times.

Even if we do not claim to have a solution for the problem of defining "reality," we are all aware that our daily lives are full of pressures. Our environment resists us. Cervantes knew the difference between this daily pressure and the lofty atmosphere of dreams: He had been a dreamer, and daily life had caught up with him. The clash between dreams and needs can be shattering. He probably intuited that the same conflict that he had experienced was also part of the pressures building up around and within the Spanish empire. His answer was twofold: irony and humor. The ironic, oblique vision gives the viewer a better sense of perspective, a more critical insight. Humor is such a basic ingredient of our existence that most of the time we do not realize how indispensable it is for our sanity—our survival. We forget thus to be grateful to those who provide it. Humor acts very much like a lubricant: it diminishes friction between the parts of our complicated psychological and social machinery. Without lubricant a motor will fall apart in minutes. A human being devoid of humor is in constant danger. The fate of a humorless society is always in doubt.

The tensions building up around his culture, and indeed around the whole Western world, have never abated. They seem to be on the rise around us in our present time. Hence Cervantes' gift is needed today more than ever. It is again a double gift: a critical, ironic insight is needed in order to organize better our societies and discover our mistakes; the gift of laughter is also indispensable in order not to despair, to see things in their proper dimensions, to rise above failure and error. Laughter is not only the best medicine, it is the only one that can see an ailing society through a period of anguish and self-doubt.

We now are aware of the fact that Cervantes achieved much more than the overthrowing of the vogue of the romances of chivalry, which undoubtedly were headed for oblivion without his help. His contemporaries were only dimly aware of the importance of his great novel. Literary criticism was then still in its infancy, and in any case it was seldom applied to contemporary works, least of all to the kind of amusing prose fiction written by Cervantes. The novel had not yet attained literary stature. Prose fiction did exist; the novel as we know it was yet unborn. When Cervantes' great novel appeared, prose fiction was instantaneously transformed: in the race to create the modern novel it can be said of Cervantes, as it was said of an American general who was also victorious, that "he got there the firstest with the mostest." The rules of the game—the game of seeing and understanding the world around the writer and his readers, of describing the interaction between characters, the evolution of human beings pitted against each other and against their own dreams—had been changed by the explosion of knowledge known as the Renaissance. As usual, only a handful of observers were aware of the importance and the meaning of the new rules. Cervantes took full advantage of his insight. He made use of dialogue to portray the inner nature of his characters, to reveal them to us in subtle ways. The interplay between vision and daily life was revealed and analyzed. In his prose fiction and his short plays, characters really talk to each other, really listen and respond—not always rationally or wisely, but this too is part of the story Cervantes unfolds. In brief, what used to be a flat and grey picture became in his works three-dimensional and colored. The world has never forgotten this feat—we are almost tempted to call it a miracle.

There is still another gift to be found in his pages: his compassion for the humble, his sense of brotherhood for every character he creates, no matter how poor, ignorant or downtrodden. Cervantes was a truly democratic writer: he realized that a peasant like Sancho Panza, a servant girl like Maritornes, a pair of urchins like Rinconete and Cortadillo, were intrinsically more interesting—more alive, more spontaneous, more charitable, loyal, and friendly—than a highborn Duke. A novelist, Cervantes seems to tell us, can afford to make many mistakes; yet there is for him an unforgivable sin, snobbishness. This lesson is perhaps easy for us to learn: it was not so in his own lifetime and for years after his death. Only in the nineteenth century, a period where his influence was to be felt everywhere, does the lesson begin to sink in. From Balzac to Dostoevski, we notice that some of the most interesting characters created by European novelists are born humble and poor. Any perceptive reader of Tolstoi's *War and Peace* will detect a family resemblance between

Platon Karataiev, the wise Russian peasant, and Sancho Panza, the far from foolish offspring of the Spanish countryside.

Writing a book about Cervantes is, for any lover of Spanish letters, an awesome challenge. One has the feeling of intruding upon a towering, almost royal presence (a feeling that would make Cervantes laugh, no doubt, but which is nonetheless real). As Lowry Nelson points out, "in those myriad couplings of the names of the great so dear to celebrants and surveyors of literature Cervantes appears ritually linked to Homer, Dante, Shakespeare, and Goethe: his is the *Spanish* niche in an official literary hall of fame."[2] The vast and ever-increasing bibliography on the subject is also a powerful deterrent: who can possibly read everything that has been written on the life and works of Cervantes? Several lifetimes entirely devoted to the task would not cover the field. Yet our view of his role, our interpretation of his works, must be constantly brought up to date. There is not, nor can there be, one single presentation of his art that could hope to supersede all others. We approach his creations as a jeweler does a diamond: we look at one side, then at another, we try to picture the whole without being able to encompass it in our field of vision.

In the preparation of the present volume I have been helped by two facts. The first one is psychological and subjective: my conviction that a succinct analysis of all the aspects of Cervantes' life and works may show their interrelationship and thus shed more light on Cervantes' masterpieces than, for instance, another learned article on an obscure point in *Don Quixote.* Our puzzle seems to be growing new pieces with each passing year. It is time to start organizing these pieces. The other fact is external: the help I have received in my research from friends, colleagues and students (I am fortunately one of those teachers, too few I am afraid, who manages to learn a considerable amount of facts and ideas from his graduate students, and indeed from his undergraduate ones). Our librarians at Yale have been as patient and cooperative as usual, which is far above the national average, I am told. Finally, my wife has helped me invaluably with translations of texts, comments, and criticism of both kinds, negative and positive. My gratitude goes to all of them.

MANUEL DURÁN

Yale University, New Haven, Connecticut

Chronology

1547   Miguel de Cervantes Saavedra is born in Alcalá de Henares, the son of Rodrigo de Cervantes and Leonor de Cortinas, fourth in a family of seven. Baptized October 9.

1551   The Franco-Spanish wars begin.

1556   Charles V, Holy Roman Emperor, abdicates.

1563   The Council of Trent (begun in 1545) ends, reaffirming dogmatic Catholic doctrine.

1568–   Poems of Cervantes published in commemoration of the
1569   death of Isabel de Valois, third wife of Philip II.

1569   Cervantes in Rome, in the service of Cardinal Giulio Acquaviva.

1571   The Christian fleet, commanded by Don John of Austria, defeats the Turks at Lepanto. Cervantes fights heroically. Twice wounded, loses the use of his left hand.

1575   After residing in Italy for some time, he sets sail on the galley *Sol*, going back to Spain. Captured by Turks and taken to Algiers as slave.

1575–   Captive in Algiers where he unsuccessfully organizes
1580   four attempts to escape with his fellow Christian prisoners.

1580   Cervantes is ransomed by a Trinitarian friar.

1581–   Cervantes attempts a literary career in Madrid as a
1587   playwright, without much success. Love affair with Ana Franca de Rojas. His daughter Isabel de Saavedra is born.

1584   Publishes a pastoral novel, *La Galatea*. Marries Catalina de Salazar y Palacios, eighteen years his junior. Resides in La Mancha.

1587   Becomes minor commissary for the Spanish Armada.

1588   Defeat of the Spanish Armada.

1597   Cervantes jailed in Seville for alleged malfeasance.

1602   Investigated again, perhaps again in jail.

1605   *Don Quixote* (Part I) is published in Madrid. Two editions published in the same year. Cervantes moves to Valladolid. Rumors about loose life of his sisters and daughter.

1609–   The Moriscos, or Spanish Moslems, are expelled from
1611   Spain.

1612   The *Exemplary Novels* are published.

1614   *Voyage to Parnassus* published. Cervantes at work on Part II of *Don Quixote*. The "false Quixote" appears.

1615   The second part of *Don Quixote* published in December. Also published in the same year: *Eight Plays and Eight New Interludes, Never Before Performed*.

1616   April 23: Cervantes dies in Madrid.

1617   Posthumous publication of *Persiles and Sigismunda*.

CHAPTER 1

Cervantes' Spain

A writer is almost by definition a special type of human being, more individualistic than his fellowmen. Yet he is also a man of his times, born and educated in a specific time and place. Cervantes' Spain appears directly or indirectly in each page Cervantes wrote, even in the texts he wrote with the aim of escaping his surroundings.

Cervantes knew the Spain of Charles V, a country at the apex of its glory and its influence, the leader of Europe under an Emperor who loved culture, fought with his armies as a valiant front-line warrior, and was endowed with a Quixotic vision of his role as a defender of the faith and the unity of Europe. Cervantes lived also under Philip II, the cautious bureaucrat who ruled his vast empire through paper work and intrigue. Finally, Cervantes wrote most of his masterpieces during the reign of Philip III, at a time when the unmistakable symptoms of the economic, military, and political decline of the mighty Spanish empire were beginning to appear.

The Spain of Charles V (1516—1556) was a country convinced of its special role, its unique destiny. Nothing was or seemed impossible to the Spaniards of that time. They had achieved, under Ferdinand and Isabella, the political unity of Castilian peoples, Catalan and Valentian regions in the Eastern seaboard, and Southern outposts of Islam. The whole of the Peninsula, with the exception of Portugal, had become united under the Castilian crown; Columbus and the explorers that followed him had taken possession of almost half the world in the name of Castile.

Each year brought news of fresh discoveries and bold conquests. Charles V was not born in Spain, but as soon as he came to Castile, still a young man, he became thoroughly Hispanicized—and dreamed of reshaping Europe along Spanish lines. A crusade was needed, or rather two crusades, one against the Moors and another

13

against the Protestants and all the forces in central Europe that did
not want to acknowledge the supremacy of the Emperor. If other
countries, such as France or England, tried to interfere, they would
have to be fought too: it was God's will and Spain's destiny.

Politics and religion went hand in hand in Charles V's Spain. The
huge investment of human energy and gold that Spain's ambitious
plans entailed had a sad consequence: the country, which was on
the verge of real prosperity, became progressively poor. Many
Spaniards left their villages and towns to fight abroad or to settle in
the newly discovered lands. Inflation accelerated. Spain needed the
gold of German and Genoese bankers: the national debt reached
colossal amounts. The dream of Charles V did not die easily: in
spite of constant troubles in Germany, in spite of the spreading of
Protestantism, the dream persisted. Victories were won, new armies
were organized, more gold was found and spent. There seemed to
be no end to the struggle. Spain sacrificed everything—the chances
for economic progress, the chances to conciliate its own dissidents,
the chances to become a modern country with respect to scientific
development—to the glorious idea of a united Europe, under one
Emperor, worshipping one God within one doctrine and one
theology. The Council of Trent, inspired by Spanish theologians
and imposed by the Spanish crown upon a reluctant Pope, was
Spain's answer—together with the founding in 1540 of the Jesuit
Order—to the growing religious anarchy.

The dream did not die under Philip II (1556–1598) even if it
meant going to war against France—who dared to encroach upon
Spanish power in Italy—and against Paul IV, the Pope, who for a
while had become the ally of France; fighting the Moors and the
Turks (who were thoroughly beaten at the naval battle of Lepanto in
1571), and fighting the Dutch who from 1566 on became the most
stubborn of Philip II's enemies. The constant, unending war in
Flanders and Holland did more than any other event to sap and
weaken the strength of Spain. On the plus side, Portugal became
(temporarily) a part of Spain, and with Portugal another vast
overseas Empire was annexed. New lands were discovered and settled, the American colonies grew more prosperous and better
organized: vast quantities of silver and gold were brought back to
Spain—only to be spent on the protracted wars of the period.

Spain was too deeply committed to the international political and religious game, half crusade and half dynastic expansion, to even think about withdrawing from it. Yet by the beginning of the seventeenth century the Spanish will was exhausted: too many wars, too many continents to settle and organize, too many changes in the intellectual horizon to be grasped and assimilated. Spain turned steadily inwards. In 1559 Philip II had forbidden Spaniards to study in foreign universities and increased the surveillance at the borders to prevent dangerous books from being introduced into the country: a long period of semi-isolation, Spain's own "Baroque Curtain," was to draw a clear line between Spain and the rest of Europe. It is true that many books printed abroad found their way into Spanish lands in spite of all precautions, and also that cultural relations with Italy were not interrupted. Yet the debilitating effects of such an attitude would jeopardize Spain's development, especially in the scientific fields, for many generations.

"Spacious and sad Spain." These are the words of a great Spanish poet of the Golden Age, Luis de León. A feeling of vastness, of empty space, is often recorded by foreign travellers in Castile during Cervantes' period. Communications were difficult (Spain had no navigable rivers, almost no man-made canals), and everything had to be carried in carts or on the back of mules. Indeed, communications were the Achilles' heel of the Spanish empire. Ships were slow and often did not reach their destination: they were waylaid by pirates or destroyed by storms. Armies advanced slowly and fought only during the months of good weather. The empire was like a huge jerry-built machine, ponderous and slow: it dwarfed the few men who tinkered with it and emitted strange clanking sounds; no part quite meshed with the others; it seemed on the verge of stopping altogether and still went on—because at the core of the machine there was a dream, and this dream would not die.

It was a beautiful dream. The world would become one, with a single monarch and a single God. The past must not be allowed to perish; it could be integrated harmoniously with the present. The Middle Ages had achieved certain spiritual goals that could and should be combined with the new Renaissance outlook. It should be reaffirmed that the Spain of the Golden Age, in giving preeminence to religious and national values, did not reject the humanistic ideas of the Renaissance nor see any incompatibility between the two of them. On the contrary. Poetry and art were to pay increasing attention to earthly values, to nature and the individual man; form was to be cultivated in the arts almost for the sake of art—and form—itself; Platonism and other types of humanism were to pervade Spanish literature. If the end product was apt to be somewhat different from what we find in other literatures, this may be due to the fact that Spanish humanism was impregnated with a peculiar Spanish characteristic, losing its predominantly pagan mood—this was the mood that prevailed in Italian humanism—and becoming juxtaposed and fused with a foundation of Medieval attitudes, much in the same way that some Renaissance churches were built upon a foundation that was still Gothic and made use of some Gothic decoration. What Philip II's Spain rejected, and by this rejection became separated from most other European countries, including Catholic countries such as France and Italy, was total freedom of investigation and scientific naturalism. Most Spanish churchmen, and not a few of Spain's intellectual leaders, thought that anything that departed radically from orthodoxy, or could put orthodoxy in jeopardy, was a menace to the newly created national unity and could plunge Spain into endless religious wars (it happened in France and Germany, and religious wars eventually would destroy Germany in the seventeenth century). New ideas were to be accepted only if they could be fitted within the framework of dogma. Of course, some fields were much less susceptible to censorship because they were intrinsically nonideological, or in any case they could embody only a limited amount of ideas: for instance, style—and illusion, illusion of all sorts. In these fields there was perfect freedom for the Spanish soul to express itself in all its complexity and all its power.

The Spaniards of the Golden Age, and more specifically of the second half of the sixteenth century, the period in which Cervantes grew up and developed as an artist, seemed to be drawn in two opposite directions: the extreme religious spiritualism of the mystics—and the extreme earthiness of the picaroons. It can be said that the picaresque is a mysticism that bears a negative sign, a minus, and plunges into total criticism of values. The mystic talks to God only seldom, and only in certain privileged moments. The picaroon does not really communicate because he does not trust anybody. He may talk, but it is only to lie and better disguise his intentions. Drawn into these two opposite directions as if by the ropes of an invisible rack, the Spanish soul remained tense, as elegant in its pain as some of the martyrs and ascetics painted by El Greco. Mystery, magic, irrationalism, belief in miracles, in the super-natural, in the constant presence of God, explain most of the irrational attitudes of that time. (Let us not forget that no national culture at that timé, not even the Dutch, was developing along pure-ly rational lines: superstition and intolerance were the norm, not the exception, all over Europe; witches and heretics were persecuted in Germany and in Massachusetts as well as in Spain.)

An air of unreality pervaded some aspects of Spanish life. Philip II sent the mighty Spanish fleet against England without any plans to exploit a possible victory by landing a Spanish army—the army was encamped in Flanders, but even if it could be spared from the war against the Dutch, no transportation had been provided for it. Only a miracle could turn the tide: was not Philip, the great sword of God, entitled to it?[1] Later on, as the situation worsened, a group of *arbitristas* (problem solvers, promoters) came to the rescue: all the devils that tormented Spain would be exorcised if only the Government followed their simple formula for success. Cervantes depicts one of those poor fellows (poor in money and luck, yet certainly rich in imagination) who claims that the King could liquidate all his debts if Spaniards would fast just once a month and hand to the Crown the money they might have otherwise spent on food. This problem-solver reminds us of another fictitious promoter who claimed that if only the English Channel were made dry (by the use of numerous huge sponges easily imported from the Orient), Spanish troops would have easy access to England. The situation was too full of paradoxes not to become frustrating: Spanish armies were still invincible by land—yet they could not deal Spain's many enemies a decisive blow; Spanish galleons brought back gold and silver—only to increase inflation and bring stagnation to Spanish in-dustry since gold allowed Spaniards to import from other countries what Spain could have manufactured.

Yet, as usual, generalizations are misleading. One cannot speak of *a* Spanish society: many groups and subgroups competed for space, power, happiness. Life in Madrid or in Seville was vastly different from life in the sleepy villages of southern Castile. Spain had ac-quired intangible assets that would endure for a long time: a sense of cohesion, common goals, above all the hope that great deeds could still be performed; in other words, a sense of grandeur and dignity, of national solidarity and acceptance of sacrifice for the common cause. Spanish soldiers grumbled but fought on. Spanish ships sailed every sea and often brought back spices and exotic foods from overseas. The geographical and intellectual horizon had been enlarged by the combination of the Renaissance and the conquest of a vast empire.

It is true that social tensions were often unbearable. Noblemen of high rank and church dignitaries could lead rich and complex lives, encompassing action and meditation, in sumptuous surroundings and with the help of armies of servants. For the petty noblemen life was less rewarding. The need to give precedence to others in the "social pecking order" led a petty nobleman in *Lazarillo de Tormes* to abandon his home town and change his address. Others found menial jobs or professions (professions were not held in high social esteem), or starved in dignity. An escape was still possible (though not for all: official permission was needed, and in the case of Cervantes was denied, we still do not know exactly why) by migrating to the colonies, preferably to the new American lands. In some obscure corners frontier life continued, with its dangers and also its rewards. Elsewhere the colonies were a haven for bureaucrats, adventurers, travelling salesmen. As long as this door was still open or ajar, social tensions could be borne: there was still hope of adventure, riches, or fame in the future of most Spaniards.

The intertwining of Church and State is perhaps the most important single characteristic of Golden Age Spain. All the arts—architecture, painting, sculpture, music—had reached a common ground: the expression of man as a spiritual being, yearning for God's grace and aware of a second higher life after the death of the body. Sinning and guilt were everywhere, but so were grace and the possibility of salvation. A stubborn sinner like Lope de Vega could also write the most passionate and sincere religious poems. Cervantes was perhaps the exception that proves the rule: he was more lay than most of his contemporaries, without, however, departing radically from the attitude and the beliefs of his times. His faith was probably as strong as theirs without being as theatrical.

The Spanish empire was too vast and far-flung not to possess a geographical and a spiritual center. It acquired both under Philip II: the Court would henceforth reside in Madrid which, with only a few brief intervals, became thus the capital and the administrative center by the King's fiat: it rises on a semiarid plain but is placed almost at the geometric center of the peninsula; El Escorial, the vast palace-church-mausoleum, where the King would retire to write his innumerable letters and memoranda—and to pray for the help of God in the execution of his vast plans—was to be the sacred city, the city of God in the Spanish plateau.

A casual modern reader might conclude that perhaps life in Golden Age Spain was too serious, even grim. He would be far from the truth. It is true that the upper classes were addicted to role-playing, they had to act their noble parts, and that could rob them of spontaneity. Private life yielded rich rewards even for them. Public life was a spectacle: church ceremonies, parades, court assemblies, as well as the work and responsibility that power entails. The theatre was an escape: Spaniards of all classes took to it as to alcohol or drugs. It was art, entertainment, ritualized presentation of socially accepted myths and conventions, all in one glamorous package. The theatre and the church were common ground for all social classes: so were the new beautiful Baroque squares, built almost like stage sets in the center of cities, where everybody could stroll, shop, talk to other people, see the lay or religious parades or take part in them and be seen by others, flirt with the unattached ladies, pick a pocket if he were a picaroon, listen to the church bells or witness a public execution or an *auto da fe*.

It may be true that the lower classes were then, as now, less inhibited about their amusements and their love life. In cities like Seville, a boom town in the sixteenth century, enriched by the trans-atlantic trade, the picaroons had almost taken over whole sections of the city: corruption was a way of life, money flowed, night life was gay. Cervantes was fond of Seville and its inhabitants: he was aware of the pettiness and cruelty of the police and courts system, and was apt to side with the transgressors rather than with the upholders of the law. In any case, he must have found the outlaws more spontaneous, sincere, and friendly than the conventional members of the middle class and the petty noblemen and bureaucrats he had to deal with most of the time. As for the writers, poets and playwrights, they proliferated in all the cities, towns, and even villages: the printing press had created a new group of readers and writers; scholarship was on the increase, and the number of poets and playwrights had never been greater. A strong tide of Platonic ideas had uplifted the generation at the beginning of the sixteenth century; an Aristotelian reaction had set in, giving important results in the field of scholastic philosophy and influencing most of the responsible literary critics. The influence of Erasmus, favorable to a religious individualism not without links with the Protestant reform, had been strong at first but had declined dramatically after a few years: yet it is probable that Cervantes was aware of the ferment created by this influence and shared some if not all of Erasmus' goals: a spirit of conciliation and common sense, a love for irony, an inner Christian faith, and a disregard for the outer pomp and ceremony. Plato and Erasmus were not the only unorthodox influences at work: outwardly Spain was a monolithic country ruled by an absolute monarch, yet a closer look reveals a rich tapestry: the last vestiges of Moorish and Hebrew culture had not disappeared completely, the independent character of Spain's provinces—the Catalans, the Basques, the Andalusians—worked against the official uniformity. And finally, if one wanted a more exotic atmosphere, it was possible to travel to Italy or to several parts of Europe without forsaking the authority or the influence of the Spanish crown. Life could be gay; freedom could be found, either by accepting wholeheartedly the official verities—or by taking refuge in the intimacy of one's thoughts, the family, a close group of friends. In spite of his irony, his criticism, his reservations, Cervantes never turned his back on the country that gave him life, education, and experience: he was a part of Spain's Golden Age and expressed it in its subtle complexities and contradictions.

CHAPTER 2

Cervantes' Harassed and Vagabond Life

W E can think of many great writers whose lives have left only a few traces upon their work. This is not so with Cervantes: his biography sheds light upon his masterpieces. He was seldom a cold and distant observer of his world: His presence as a witness and occasionally as a judge of what he saw is discreet yet undeniable. He made good use of his experience: he went so far as to include himself, as a minor character, in several of his works—much in the same way as one of our contemporary film directors, Alfred Hitchcock, appears fleetingly in his own movies. His presence is discreet yet insistent: he will not deny or betray his own personality; he begs us to take it into account when reading his texts. Pride and humility go hand in hand in him, helping him to become a good witness of his time—and of the human condition of all time.

Cervantes was born in Alcalá de Henares, a small university city not far from Madrid, in 1547, probably on September 29, St. Michael's day, since it was often the custom to bestow the name of the saint in the calendar upon a child born on that day. He was baptized in the church of Santa María la Mayor on Sunday, October 9.

His father, Rodrigo de Cervantes, was an impecunious hidalgo. He had become a practical surgeon after a few months of hurried studies at the University of Alcalá, where he had excellent friends among the medical faculty; not too long after acquiring his degree, Rodrigo married (in 1543) Leonor de Cortinas, a young girl born in Barajas, near Madrid, also a member of the gentry, also impecunious. They had seven children, all but the last two born in Alcalá de Henares.

Nothing is known about the first years of Miguel de Cervantes' life except that his family moved often. Miguel was only three and a half years old when his family moved away from Alcalá de Henares. The family was going through a period of hardship. Rodrigo's income was meager. With nine mouths to feed and little or no income, the family moved to Valladolid. Debts accumulated: Miguel's father went to jail for a few months. We find the family in Córdoba (where they settled in 1553); Córdoba was but a shadow of its former size and opulent past under the Moors, but it must still have been a fascinating city. It is in Córdoba that Miguel de Cervantes went to an elementary school (he was seven years old when his family settled there) and acquired the rudiments of learning, perhaps at the school conducted by Father Alonso de Vieras. Later on, in 1555, he probably began the study of Latin at the Jesuit College of Santa Catalina. But 1557 was a bad year: the family was pressed by debts. There is no trace of Rodrigo and his family from that date until they reappear in Seville in 1564. Miguel was by then a handsome youth of seventeen. He must have enjoyed life in Seville, then on the verge of becoming a "boom town." He probably continued his studies at the Jesuit College. Much later, one of his characters, the wise dog Ciprión, would state: "I have heard it said [he describes the Jesuit teachers at Seville] of those saintly ones that in the matter of prudence there is not their like in the world, while as guides and leaders along the heavenly path few can come up to them. They are mirrors in which are to be viewed human decency, Catholic doctrine, and extraordinary wisdom, and, lastly, a profound humility that is the basis upon which the entire edifice of a holy life is reared."[1] Later, Cervantes would describe the agreeable character of student life: "In short, I led the life of a student, without hunger and without the itch—and I can give it no higher praise than that. For if it were not that the itch and hunger are the student's constant companions, there would be no life that is pleasanter or more enjoyable, since virtue and pleasure here go hand in hand, and the young find diversion even as they learn."[2] Miguel loved to read: he was a voracious reader, and we may assume that his long lasting love affair with literature had already begun. The theatre fascinated him: it must have been a glorious day for him when Lope de Rueda, a famous actor who also wrote plays (among them his famous *pasos*, one-act plays or curtain raisers, that the modern reader finds still fresh and amusing) came to Seville and gave several performances there. This took place probably in 1564. In a prologue he later wrote to a collection of his own plays, he reminisces about that happy day. He is discussing the theatre in general, and his own childhood memories, with some of his friends: "I, as the oldest one there, said that I remembered having seen on the stage the great Lope de Rueda, a man distinguished in both acting and understanding. He was a native of Seville, and a goldsmith by trade, which means he was one of those that make gold leaf. He was admirable in pastoral poetry; and in this genre neither then nor since has anybody surpassed him."[3]

Bad luck once more besieged Cervantes' family. A certain Rodrigo de Chaves instituted a suit against Rodrigo, his father, and attached his goods. The family moved to Madrid in 1566. Miguel was now twenty. He probably continued his education there with private tutors and at the City School of Madrid under the learned López de Hoyos, who, as a follower of Erasmus, may have inculcated in his young pupil some of Erasmus' progressive and liberal ideas. Cervantes' culture was becoming broader and more solid. Nevertheless, as Richard L. Predmore states in his biography, "by the most generous estimate that the available facts will allow, young Cervantes cannot have enjoyed much more than six years of formal schooling. In most men this amount of study could not have created a sufficient base for the very considerable literary culture visible in Miguel's later writings, which reveal a good knowledge of the outstanding Latin authors, a smattering of Greek literature, a close familiarity with some of the great writers of the Italian Renaissance and the kind of acquaintance with his own literature that one might expect a boy with strong literary inclinations to possess. What he knew of the Latin language and literature was certainly grounded in his schooling; the rest must have been the product of his own reading. The five years he was soon to spend in Italy contributed decisively to his continued education and account for his extensive reading in Italian literature."[4]

At twenty Cervantes had a wandering spirit, which had been formed in his adolescence perhaps by his frequent travels through Spain. He also felt an intense yearning for both knowledge and freedom. All of this undoubtedly influenced his decision to go to Italy, which was then the mecca of all lovers of culture and of a free life. Nevertheless his trip to Italy may well have been the result of less lofty goals: it has been suggested that at this time Miguel first ran afoul of the law—since there exists in the General Record Office in Simancas a document dated September, 1569, which begins thus: "An Order of Arrest against Miguel de Cervantes. Without Right to Appeal. [signed by] Secretary Padreda. [Motive] A Crime." According to the document, he had stabbed a certain Antonio de Segura in Madrid during a challenge to a duel. No one knows for sure whether the Miguel de Cervantes alluded to in this document is *our* Miguel de Cervantes. The biographer Luis Astrana Marín, in his six learned volumes on the life of Cervantes, thinks this to be the case. In support of his charge, he cites in particular a verse of the *Voyage to Parnassus* in which the author confesses to a "youthful imprudence," from which many of his later misfortunes ensued. It is not wholly clear that we should pay much attention to this accusation, whether truly directed against our writer or not. If true, even if we conclude that Cervantes was guilty, it would only be a question of confirming one more trial, or rather one more accusation, of the many that the writer endured throughout his life. Finally, "it would not be defaming the author to admit that on occasion he was quick to reach for his sword. A gentleman at that time never went forth without strapping on his sword, and its purpose was not simply for display alone."[5]

Towards 1569 we find Cervantes in Italy, where he had travelled as a member of the retinue of Cardinal Acquaviva. Shortly afterwards he enlisted in the Spanish army and was sent to sea. He fought heroically under the command of Don John of Austria in the sea battle of Lepanto in 1571 and was twice wounded: one wound paralyzed his left hand. He later took part in other campaigns, especially the raids against Tunis and the nearby fortress of La Goleta. In 1575 he embarked for Spain with his brother Rodrigo.[6] He carried with him warm letters of recommendation from his superiors. The galley in which he travelled was seized by Turkish pirates. Thus began five years of captivity, as a slave to his captor, the Greek renegade Dali Mamí. At the end of this period, and after several frustrated attempts to escape, he was ransomed by some Trinitarian monks and was able to return to Spain. Thus Cervantes had passed some twelve years outside Spain—and these were the decisive years in the life of any man, the years between twenty and thirty-three. He returned enriched by his experience; his thirst for adventure had been partially quenched; he longed for stability, a career, some kind of stable success. Success, however, was to prove out of reach.

When he returned to Spain in 1680, several unpleasant experiences still awaited him. He soon realized there was no hope of obtaining any reward for his services. A military career seemed hopeless since one of his arms was no longer useful. Thus began a ceaseless struggle against poverty and neglect. First he lived in Madrid, then he moved to Portugal for a short time. He found no place to root himself. He became a writer almost out of desperation: what else could he do? How could he earn a living? He began to write out of love for literature but also, probably, out of desperation, hoping to find in his literary career a source of income. He was thus from the very beginning a professional writer, although an unsuccessful one at first. The most popular genres were then the pastoral novel and the theater: he tried them both to little avail. A brief love affair made him a father: an illegitimate daughter, Isabel de Saavedra, was the consequence of his affair. In 1584 he married Catalina de Salazar, a woman somewhat younger than himself, and it seems that he found no happiness in his marriage. He lived for a time in Esquivias, a village of La Mancha where his wife had a farm. It was the heart of arid Spain, a poor land almost impossible to idealize: its inhabitants were ignorant and backward. From his memories of life in La Mancha, he would later create Don Quixote and his environment. Cervantes then turned to humble jobs, since literature had proved incapable of providing him with a living. He became quartermaster for the Invincible Armada: for ten years he was an itinerant buyer, living in Seville and other towns in Andalusia. He had separated from his wife, whom he never mentioned in his works. In 1597, because of the bankruptcy of a financier with whom he had deposited some state funds, he was jailed in Seville. In these years he became acquainted with people of the lower class: it seems obvious that he found them more outgoing and decent than the people of the middle and upper classes with whom he had dealings. He did not lack for occasion to study at first hand the myriad forms of picaresque life, since Seville was the capital of the picaroons. The city was growing fast, having become the economic center of Spain and the main port of the overseas fleets. Gold and silver poured into Spain from Seville. Industry flourished. Rapid growth and change—plus a transient population—made for a minimum of social constraints. It is in Seville that Cervantes must have known the real-life counterpart of Monipodio, the good-tempered, humane Al Capone of the Golden Age.

There was another Spain, much less glamorous than the pageant of Seville, that also attracted his attention: life in the villages of Andalusia and along the winding, sun-drenched roads leading to these villages. Cervantes came to know it well: the poor inns, the wandering artisans and shepherds, the long convoys of mule trains, the humble yet proud peasants. It was another strand in the huge tapestry that unfolded before him. Cervantes was the perfect witness, observing every detail, noticing the delicate balance and the constant interaction between human beings, taking mental notes about their foibles and their moments of happiness.

Life was never boring. Yet Cervantes was always on the verge of bankruptcy: he was not a businessman, his records were not accurate, the financial rewards of his jobs were meager. It is not surprising, therefore, that in 1590 he petitioned to find a position in the Spanish colonies overseas. His hopes were dashed: an ungrateful administration rejected his petition. Perhaps his troubles with the law had convinced the bureaucrats that he was basically unreliable. Cervantes had pleaded: "Sire: Miguel de Cervantes Saavedra says that he has served Your Majesty for many years in the sea and land campaigns that have occurred over the last 22 years, particularly in the Naval Battle [Lepanto], where he received many wounds, among which was the loss of a hand from gunfire . . . and he has since continued to serve in Seville on business of the Armada, under the orders of Antonio de Guevara, as is on record in the testimonials in his possession. In all this time he has received no favors at all. He asks and begs as humbly as he can that Your Majesty be pleased to grant him the favor of a position in America, of the three or four currently vacant, namely, the accountant's office in the new Kingdom of Granada, or the governorship of the province of Soconusco in Guatemala, or the office of ship's accountant in Cartagena, or that of corregidor in the city of La Paz . . ."[7] As Richard Predmore observes, "influence and money won more jobs than merit, it seems. On 6 June 1590, an official of the Council of the Indies scribbled on the back of Cervantes' memorial: 'Let him look on this side of the water for some favor that may be granted him.' Perhaps the sympathetic reader will console himself with the proverb about the ill wind that blows no good. The action of the

Council of the Indies unwittingly favored the birth of Don Quixote."[8]

There can be no doubt about Cervantes' honesty. Each new supervisor confirmed him in his job. There can be doubt either about his bad luck. In 1602 he was again, for a short time, in jail at Seville. In 1604 he decided to move to Valladolid. The decisive moment was at hand: early in 1605 the first part of *Don Quixote* appeared. Yet Cervantes' joy at the instantaneous success of his novel was short-lived. Again he became involved with the police: a gentleman, Gaspar de Ezpeleta, was fatally wounded in a duel at the entrance of Cervantes' house. The investigation proved Cervantes and his family had nothing to do with this incident—yet it also revealed that Cervantes' sister and daughter led somewhat irregular lives, were frequently visited by male friends and received gifts from them.

Cervantes' huge literary success did not bring him riches: his publisher and several pirate publishers kept most of the profits. But it did motivate him to go on writing.

In 1606 the Court settled again in Madrid: Cervantes and his family moved with it. Cervantes wanted to be in touch with other writers and was looking for new publishers; the women in his household, busy with fashion designing and sewing, were looking for customers. Miguel's last years in Madrid were relatively serene. He overcame through patience and wisdom all his adversities, the neglect of famous writers such as Lope de Vega—who seldom had a good word for his works—and the sadness of family crises: his daughter married but soon became the mistress of a wealthy middle-aged businessman; when Cervantes intervened in the interest of preventing scandal, she became estranged and never again visited him. Cervantes immersed himself in his work. It was harvest season for him: late in life, yet in full command of his talent, he produced in quick succession his *Exemplary Novels* (1613), the second part of *Don Quixote* (1615), and finally *Persiles and Sigismunda*, a novel in which his imagination and his love for adventure found almost limitless scope. Cervantes knew his days were numbered. He suffered from a disease which was diagnosed as dropsy—some modern biographers think it was diabetes—and had to stay in bed for long periods. He could not stop writing until the very end. Early in April, 1616, his doctor recommended a trip to Esquivias, in the hope that

country air would reinvigorate him. On April 19 he was back in
Madrid: he busied himself with the final pages of his *Persiles* and the
Prologue to the novel. In the Prologue he describes an encounter
with a student on his way back from his recent visit to Esquivias. The
student is very pleased to meet, as he says, "the famous one, the
merry author, the jubilation of the Muses." They ride along for a
while and the conversation turns to Cervantes' health. The student
diagnoses Cervantes' disease as "dropsy" and advises him to curb his
drinking. He replies, "Many have told me . . . but I find it as difficult not to drink my fill as though I had been born for that purpose
alone. My life is coming to an end, and by the tempo of my pulse
beats, I judge that their career and mine will be over on Sunday at
the latest." He goes on to describe the parting of the new friends and
closes with a general farewell: "Farewell to the Graces, farewell to
wit, farewell to cheerful friends, for I am dying in the desire to see
you soon contented in the other life."[9] He died in Madrid on April
23, 1616, at peace with himself and with the world, having received
the last sacraments, and was buried in the convent of the Trinitarian
nuns. He died without bitterness or regrets since he had been fully
conscious of his merit, indeed of his genius, and was aware that his
literary creations would endure: a writer cannot hope for a greater
source of consolation.

   Objectively, Cervantes' life was not a success story. He was
seldom in full control: he was too poor; for many years he lacked
public recognition. Yet, as Angel del Río points out, "there is no
reason to lament Cervantes' misfortunes nor the mediocrity of his
daily life. He could thus, through an experience which is seldom obtained when the writer is successful and wealthy, know, observe and
feel the beat of Spanish life in its greatness and its poverty, in its
heroic fantasy and in the sad reality of an imminent decadence. He
was to leave in his books the most faithful image of this life, reflected
in multiple perspectives with bittersweet irony and penetrating
humor."[10]

   If Cervantes' biography teaches us anything, it is that he was at
the same time *inside* and *outside* the mainstream of Spanish life. As
an insider, he took part in the battle of Lepanto and wrote at least
two successful books, *Don Quixote* and the *Exemplary Novels*. This
is certainly much more than the level of achievement of most
middle-class hidalgos of his time. As an outsider, he was always

poor—almost to the point of being destitute—and not infrequently in jail; he lacked influential friends in a society where nothing could be done without them and without money; he was often unable to protect adequately the female members of his family; the influential critics and writers of his time did not recognize the quality of his work; his accomplishments as a soldier and as a loyal member of the Administration were ignored—while his every minor transgression was punished harshly. A complete outsider would have rebelled or subsided into depression and silence. A complete insider would have seen only the rosiest aspects of Spanish life. It was his fate, and our gain, that he saw both sides. Out of his twofold experience a complex picture of Spanish society was born. It was a picture that included irony and parody, idealism and criticism, realism and fantasy: it was so rich and complex that we can still see ourselves mirrored in it. This is what makes him a classic. He knew that criticism without love created a distorted image, love without criticism a bland, fuzzy image. Luckily for him—and for us—he was plentifully endowed with a critical eye and a compassionate heart.

A last footnote to his biography seems necessary, so much the more as most of his biographers (and this is the case even with his most recent ones, such as Richard Predmore) have chosen to ignore or neglect this point. It is a mere detail, almost meaningless to the modern reader, yet all-important to the inhabitant of Golden Age Spain: was Cervantes an "old Christian"? In other words, are we sure (and was he sure) that he did not belong to a "New Christian" family, a *converso* family, in other words, a family in which some ancestors were converted Jews? A critical, ironic bent, plus an affinity for the ideas of Erasmus seem to point in the direction of a *converso* ancestry. The documentary proofs are lacking. Yet some of the best modern Hispanists, Américo Castro and Stephen Gilman among them, lean towards the idea that Cervantes came from a *converso* family. As Gilman states, "Salvador de Madariaga was first to give printed expression to a suspicion that those readers who had perceived Cervantes' constant mockery of pretensions to lineage (not only in the *Retablo de las maravillas* [*The Marvelous Pageant*], but also in the *Persiles* and the *Quixote*) had fleetingly entertained . . . . Since then Castro in his *Cervantes y los casticismos* (*Cervantes and the Caste System*), Madrid, 1966, has brought additional information to the fore . . . . The presence of no less than five

physicians in Cervantes' immediate family will seem highly significant to those familiar with the social history of the time."[11] We may
never know for certain. If these suspicions were to be confirmed,
they would help to explain Cervantes' official neglect, his failure to
achieve social status, his ironic vision. Be it as it may, he was a
"marginal man," according to the sociologists' cliché, and his work
bears witness to this fact. Of course, a "marginal man" usually
becomes a humorist—when at all possible, if bitterness or depression
do not interfere. This was his case. His merry vision transcended
each personal crisis, each disappointment. His robust laughter and
his ironic smile can still help us to achieve the same goals.

CHAPTER 3

Cervantes as a Poet

I *A Frustrated Dream*

C ERVANTES'S first literary composition was a poem, an elegy
written on the occasion of the Queen's death. Isabel of Valois,
Philip II's wife, died in 1568. Cervantes was then twenty-one years
old. From that moment on, he would never cease writing poetry. His
ambition was to become a first-rate poet, as well as a good
playwright and a proficient novelist. Poetry was his first love, and
the fact that he seldom succeeded in writing poetry that pleased
either himself or his readers was a constant source of distress. Cervantes was too intelligent and sensitive not to realize his own shortcomings as a poet:

> *Yo, que siempre trabajo y me desvelo*
> *Por parecer que tengo de poeta*
> *La gracia que no quiso darme el cielo . . .*[1]

> (I, ever busy, ever losing sleep
> In order to appear as if I had the poetic gift
> that Heaven would not give me . . .)

He would write this near the end of his life in his *Voyage to Parnassus*. The great reputation of Cervantes as a prose writer has
always been an obstacle towards the proper evaluation of his poetic
production. His output as a poet was not a meager one. Ten of his
longest dramas and two of his *Interludes* are written in verse form,
aside from the many compositions found throughout his novels and
the poems he contributed to anthologies. Cervantes was well acquainted with traditional Spanish forms, such as the *romance* or
ballad, the *villancico* or Christmas song, etc. He was also familiar

31

with the new Italianate fashion introduced by Garcilaso de la Vega
during the first half of the sixteenth century. Garcilaso's poetry is
musical, supple, mysterious; it brings to our mind the poetry of
Vergil and Petrarch. Cervantes's poetry is often more narrative and
less lyrical than his model. Yet there can be no doubt as to Cervantes' ideal poet: he praises Garcilaso time and time again, even
finds a way to introduce his books incidentally in his own novels.
Thus one of the characters in Cervantes' *Persiles* quotes Garcilaso
and praises him profusely, and when the hero of the *novella, El
Licenciado Vidriera (The Glass Scholar)*, decides to give up his life as
a student, he gets rid of all his books but two, a book of prayers and a
book of poems by Garcilaso.

Cervantes' first attempt at the novel, *La Galatea*, afforded him the
opportunity to write numerous poems. The plot involved all the ingredients of the pastoral, shepherds and shepherdesses in and out of
love: each incident had to be celebrated, if love was triumphant, by
a poem, or, if love was unrequited, lamented by a poetic composition. Yet these pastoral poems are on the whole stiff and add very little to the novel's artistic climate: one is almost forced to the conclusion that Cervantes' prose is here more musical and full of rhythm
than his songs and sonnets. His love for bucolic poetry never disappeared altogether and would find new outlets in *Don Quixote*, especially in the pastoral section where Crisóstomo, a rejected
pseudoshepherd, sings his distress.

Another aspect of poetry beckoned: epic poetry. The period was
one of tenacious struggles, great battles, remarkable feats of valor.
Cervantes himself had been a hero: he had fought bravely at Lepanto and would never forget it. A Spaniard, the gifted Fernando de
Herrera, "Divine Herrera" as many readers called him, had proved
that one did not necessarily have to write a whole epic poem in order
to become an epic poet; a longish poem on a lofty subject would suffice. Cervantes probably felt on firmer ground when tackling such a
task. He had seen battle at first hand; he had smelled gunpowder
and heard the whistling of cannon balls. Epic poetry was worth trying. The subject at hand was relevant, the expedition of the Spanish
Armada.

Two long poems came out of this effort. The first was actually
written, at least in part, before the Armada sailed, and its keynote is
enthusiasm. He imagines the swift sword of the Spanish warriors

shining in the fog, the war machines filling the air with noise and destruction, ships accosting other ships, flags flapping in the wind. The *Second Song to the Invincible Armada* was written after the news of the Spanish fleet's destruction had reached Spain. Its tone is somber, bitter, almost despairing. The poet addresses Philip II and reminds him of the everincreasing dangers, bringing the sovereign—and himself—down to earth:

> *Tus puertos salteados*
> *en las remotas Indias apartadas,*
> *y en tus casas tus naves abrasadas*
> *y en la ajena los templos profanados;*
> *tus mares llenos de piratas fieros;*
> *por ellos, tus armadas encogidas;*
> *y en ellos mil haciendas y mil vidas*
> *sujetas a mil bárbaros aceros . . .*[2]

> (Your seaports plundered
> in the remote distant Indies
> and at home your ships burned
> and elsewhere the temples profaned;
> your seas full of fierce pirates,
> throughout them your armadas shrunken
> and on them a thousand fortunes and a thousand lives
> subject to a thousand barbarous blades . . .)

Also a favorite theme of Cervantes is the naval battle of Lepanto, which he remembers in his *Journey to Parnassus* and in his "Letter to Mateo Vázquez":

> *Vi el formado escuadrón roto y deshecho,*
> *y de bárbara gente y de cristiana*
> *rojo en mil partes de Neptuno el lecho.*[3]

> (I saw the ships' formation broken, destroyed,
> and Neptune's bed reddened in a thousand places
> by barbarians and Christians.)

This "Letter to Mateo Vázquez," written during Cervantes' captivity in Algiers, is notable for the wealth of autobiographical elements which it contains and for the loftiness of its feeling. But its

strictly poetic value is very uneven. In no moment does it attain the
emotional impact which Cervantes' predicament might have inspired.

If Heaven had not seen fit to bless Cervantes with the gift of true
poetic grace, the answer was obviously in hard work, in trying time
and time again. He read Garcilaso, Luis de León, Fernando de
Herrera; he also listened to folk singers, balladeers, traditional oral
poets. Poetry was the queen of the arts, the first of all literary genres.
Cervantes, as a professional writer trying to "project an image,"
could not ignore this supreme art. Yet his talent pulled him in other
directions. Perhaps the reason he could not fully succeed as a poet
was a psychological one: he refused to reveal his inner self—and
without such a commitment true lyrical poetry becomes impossible.
Cervantes seldom discusses his innermost feelings; when he does, it
is in such an oblique fashion that the reader has to guess what he is
hinting at.

Often a great poem gives the reader the impression that the poet
has been able to take hold of the flow of time, slowing it down at will
in order to show us the interaction between the external beauty of
the world and the internal reaction of one individual. Memory, emotion, and images interact: A new, complex inner truth is revealed.
This process affords us a glimpse of the poet's inner self—and at the
same time reveals a new facet of the world that surrounds him. Cervantes would not or perhaps could not play this game: his inner self
had to be protected at all costs from the gaze of his readers. His
talent was projected towards the narrative, towards a flow of events
in which other individuals would reveal their inner selves through
their thoughts and conversations, and by interacting with each
other. In other words, Cervantes always thought of literature in
terms of fiction, even when writing poetry. It is difficult, nearly impossible, to be a good fiction writer and a good lyrical poet at
the same time. There are a few examples of great writers who
have managed to be both. The names of Pushkin, of
D. H. Lawrence, of Poe and Hugo come to mind. Closer to Cervantes, Quevedo had succeeded in both fiction and poetry. Yet the
qualities needed for writing good narrative prose are basically so
different from the qualities a good poet needs in his art that the coincidence of these two talents is nearly impossible. Quevedo's fiction
created characters less developed than Cervantes' novels: stiff, one-

sided, almost mechanical.

Cervantes' model was, as we have stated, Garcilaso de la Vega; Cervantes' rival, the man who occupied the center of the stage in Spanish letters, was Lope de Vega. Both Garcilaso and Lope de Vega were true poets, poets speaking to the human heart, the human emotions, through musical language and subtle yet powerful images. Both revealed their inner selves while writing poetry. Cervantes did not. His poems tell us nothing about his inner world, his love or lack of love for his wife or any other woman, his feelings of elation, anger, or despair when faced with important events in his own existence or in the life of his friends, his enemies, the small world in which he moved. He remained to the end extremely discreet, almost secretive, with respect to his private life, the opposite, thus, of Lope de Vega, who paraded in his poems, letters, and conversations his complicated and stormy love life. It is no wonder, therefore, that Lope de Vega should feel a certain contempt for Cervantes, a man who tried his hand at poetry without the necessary emotional attitude to be successful at it.

II *Cervantes' Major Effort, his* Voyage to Parnassus

In 1614, near the end of his life, Cervantes published in Madrid a long poem, *Viaje del Parnaso (Voyage to Parnassus)*, basically an imitation of the Italian poem, *Viaggio in Parnasso*, by a second-rate Tuscan poet, Cesare Caporali di Perugia (1531–1601). Cervantes' poem is composed of more than a thousand three-line stanzas or *tercetos*. Cervantes develops the same allegory as the Italian poet: the incompetent poets attempt to climb the summit of Mount Parnassus, the abode of the Muses. In response to this, and by order of Apollo, Mercury undertakes a trip to Spain—one which Cervantes describes in minute detail—in search of true poets. This is followed by the eulogies to some hundred Spanish poets who go off with Mercury towards Parnassus. Cervantes' eulogies are on the whole boring, monotonous, redundant. There is a wealth of praises, although concealed beneath them we can detect a note of sadness, a certain irony, and even some resentment. Cervantes regrets that he is not being included among the select group of travellers, and mentions some of his poetic works almost as if he wished to change Mercury's mind. In the symbolic galley in which the trip is to take place, the poets gather and converse. They journey along the Italian coasts and

finally arrive in front of the magic mountain and begin to climb it.
At the same time there also arrives another ship loaded with poets
who are complaining that Cervantes has not included them in the
voyage, and with respect to these new arrivals Cervantes laments:

> *Unos, porque los puse, me abominan;*
> *Otros, porque he dejado de ponellos,*
> *De darme pesadumbre determinan.*
>
> *Yo no sé cómo me avendré con ellos:*
> *Los puestos se lamentan; los no puestos*
> *Gritan; yo tiemblo destos y de aquellos.*[4]
>
> (Some, because I included them, detest me;
> Others, because I did not include them
> Determine to give me grief.
>
> I do not know how I will manage with them:
> The chosen ones lament, the discarded ones
> Scream; I tremble before them both.)

But the newly arrived vessel is sunk in the sea by order of Nep-
tune, and Venus, dressed in current fashion, appears and changes
them all into huge pumpkins and wineskins. Apollo then addresses
words of encouragement to his poets: a battle is joined. The incompetent poets, grotesque in their new shapes, fire into the ranks of
the good poets their heavy volumes, but are finally defeated and put
to flight. All these events serve by way of preface to the opinion of
Cervantes with respect to his contemporary spinners of rhyme.
Apollo believes that only nine great poets are worthy of the crown to
be awarded, and this occasions enormous displeasure among the
crowd of poets. Who are these poets? Cervantes only hints. Perhaps
Quevedo, the two Argensola brothers, and then we seem to draw a
blank: a mood of suspense has been created.

The *Voyage to Parnassus* is an uneven poem. Some of its lines
compare with the best in the tradition of Golden Age poetry, such as
this description of the poet's art, or perhaps a definition of the beauty of poetry in general:

> *La mayor hermosura se deshace*
> *ante ella, y ella sola resplandece*
> *sobre todas, alegra y satisface.*
>
> *Bien así semejaba cual se ofrece*
> *entre líquidas perlas y entre rosas*
> *la Aurora que despunta y amanece.*[5]

> (The greatest beauty is overshadowed
> before it, and it alone is resplendent.
> It gives joy and satisfaction more than anything else.
>
> Dawn is just as beautiful as it appears
> among liquid pearls and among roses
> as it arises bringing a new day.)

Yet some of the lines and even some of the stanzas are harsh to the ear and are occasionally prosaic. Cervantes' genius has been unable on the whole to rise above the poetic clichés of his period. The work ends with an addendum in prose which is strikingly better than the poem itself.

Obviously, the composition of such a long poem, at a time when Cervantes was old and not in good health, must have taxed his strength. The financial reward to be obtained was going to be—Cervantes could well imagine—either meager or nonexistent. Why, then, did he write it? The answer that comes to mind is that the *Voyage to Parnassus* was planned and executed as an exercise in what we would at present call "public relations." Cervantes, by 1614, had already become well known, even famous, among the many readers of the first part of *Don Quixote*. Yet the literary establishment had not accepted him as a first-rank writer. It was necessary to remind the most influential Spanish authors that he was still alive, still capable of writing long poems, and moreover capable of writing literary criticism—or rather the type of abundant praise and occasional ironic negative comments that passed for literary criticism in the seventeeth century.

We see Cervantes in the midst of a crowd of poets, mostly Spanish poets, and he seems to know them all, has a sentence or a couple of adjectives that define each poet and his works, and in a word seems to belong in this crowd, although his irony and occasional bitterness make the reader aware that he is at best a marginal poet among the illustrious names he mentions. Cervantes, persistent, even stubborn in his wish to be read and liked, seems to tell his contemporaries that he is still in the running, has not retired from the literary competitions, and is still capable of writing in several genres: novel, short story, theatre, poetry. As a professional writer, Cervantes wanted to write a poem that would make his presence felt once more, a poem in which he could list his accomplishments and complain, in a self-deprecating mood, of the fact that most of what he had published so far had been received coldly by Spain's literary elite.

III   *A Touch of Irony, a Touch of Pathos*

Cervantes' greatest asset as a poet is perhaps his occasional but effective use of irony. This can be clearly seen in a sonnet dealing with the "rescue" of the port of Cadiz by the Duke of Medina Sidonia. In July, 1596, a British fleet under the command of Lord Howard of Effingham and the Earl of Essex had attacked Cadiz, taken the fortress, plundered the city, sunk numerous Spanish ships. After a few days of indecision and panic, the Spanish troops came back to a city in ruins. Cervantes describes first the truculent parade of Spanish troops in Seville: the soldiers wear gaudy costumes, plumed hats, are armed to the teeth, and frighten the populace; it is a theatrical parade, very much like the one during the Holy Week. In the meantime, Cadiz burns and is plundered. Finally the comic, ironic anticlimax takes place: the English depart, after having occupied the Spanish port during twenty-four days, and only then the Spaniards retake their city:

> y al cabo, en Cádiz, con mesura harta,
> ido ya el conde sin ningún recelo,
> triunfando entró el gran duque de Medina.[6]

(and at last the great Duke of Medina
since Essex had departed without fear
slowly, very slowly entered triumphant in Cadiz.)

What is most remarkable in this sonnet is not the irony in itself, but the daring with which Cervantes deals with a painful subject, one which brought back to any Spanish reader the memory of the defeat of the Armada through the incompetence of Medina Sidonia, the memory of the first attack on Cadiz by Drake, and finally the memory of this second ignominious defeat of the Spanish army against Howard's ships and Essex' troops. Cervantes' irony becomes here black humor.

Grief and pathos appear less often than irony and humor in Cervantes' poems. Perhaps the foremost example of sadness, almost to the brink of despair, can be found in the already mentioned "Letter to Mateo Vázquez," which he wrote during his captivity in North Africa. It is an uneven poem, probably written in haste under the suspicious eyes of his jailers. The poem is addressed to Mateo Vázquez de Leca (1542–1591), a powerful man—he was Philip II's Secretary—who, it was gossiped at that time, had been born in Algiers to a captive Spanish woman, and therefore could understand better than most the plight of the Spanish prisoners in North Africa. After addressing Vázquez, Cervantes begs Philip II to come to the rescue of the captives by sending a fleet and landing an army. The Moors, he claims, are not well armed; they will flee if attacked; the Christians are many, their sufferings have become unbearable:

> Cada uno mira si tu armada viene,
> para dar a sus pies el cargo y cura
> de conservar la vida que sostiene.
>
> Del amarga prisión triste y oscura
> adonde mueren veinte mil cristianos
> tienes la llave de su cerradura.
>
> Todos, cual yo, de allá puestas las manos,
> las rodillas por tierra, sollozando,
> cercados de tormentos inhumanos,
>
> valeroso señor, te están rogando
> vuelvas los ojos de misericordia
> a los suyos, que están siempre llorando.[7]
>
> (Each one looks out to see if your armada is coming
> in order to charge their feet
> to preserve the life that sustains them.

Of this bitter, sad and dark prison
where twenty thousand Christians are dying
you hold the key to its lock.

All, like myself, with hands outstretched,
on bended knees, sobbing,
beset by merciless torments,

worthy lord, they are begging you
to turn your merciful eyes
to theirs, which are always in tears.)

The poem ends in one pathetic line. It is interrupted here, when his jailers seize him:

y al trabajo me llaman donde muero[8]
(and they call me to the work where I shall die.)

Yet, in spite of these moments of emotion, it cannot be said that the "Letter to Mateo Vázquez" is a great poem. Flashes of insight, pathos, or irony abound in Cervantes' poetry—yet true lyrical greatness eluded him. He knew the rules of the game, but was seldom a winner. Ever the true professional in other literary genres, the inescapable conclusion is that when he wrote poetry he was at best a gifted amateur.

CHAPTER 4

Cervantes as a Playwright

I An Enduring Love

W HEN Cervantes came back to Spain in 1580 after five years of captivity in Algiers, the future looked bleak. He was penniless. The wounds received during his years as a soldier made it impossible to pursue a military career: his left arm was paralyzed. He had lost contact with his friends. He did not know where to turn for gainful employment.

Only literature beckoned. In literature the theatre was the most popular genre at the moment; therefore, the writing of plays attracted him strongly. He had been interested in the theatre since his early schooldays. Given his fondness for the theatre and the fact that it offered a promising future for a young writer, it was almost unavoidable that he should try his hand at writing plays.

When towards the end of his life Cervantes published some of his plays, he wrote a preface in which he describes his beginnings as a playwright: "The theatres of Madrid saw performed *The Manners of Algiers*, *The Destruction of Numantia*, and *The Naval Combat*, in which I dared to reduce comedies to three acts, from the five they used to have; I showed, or rather, I was the first to represent the imaginings and secret thoughts of the soul, setting moral figures on the stage to the general and pleasurable applause of the listeners. I composed at that time up to twenty or thirty plays, all of which were received without cucumbers or other things suitable for throwing; they enjoyed their run without whistling, shouting or hubbub. I had other things with which to busy myself; I put aside my pen and my plays; and then that monster of nature, the great Lope de Vega, entered the scene and made off with the crown of the comic monarchy."[1]

There is some sadness in Cervantes' comments. He thought

highly about his own plays (in a contract he signed with a producer, he stipulated that, if after the first performances it appeared Cervantes' play was not "one of the best ever performed in Spain," the producer would get his money back, that is to say, Cervantes believed so much in the excellence of his play that he sold it with a "money back guarantee"), yet as soon as literary fashions changed, Lope de Vega outshone Cervantes as a playwright and Cervantes could never again aspire to a leading role in the Spanish stage.

Yet Cervantes' love for the theatre did not disappear. We can see this love, for instance, in the long passages of criticism dealing with the theatre that he inserted in *Don Quixote* (in Part I, Chapters 49—50). Towards the end of his life he wrote several short plays, and gathered eight comedies and eight one-act plays in one volume. It appeared in Madrid in 1615. Perhaps this book was a challenge to Lope. Lope was the undisputed king of the Spanish stage—but Cervantes wanted to establish his own independent fiefdom. Not without reason: it seems obvious, at least from the vantage point of modern criticism, that Cervantes was in his youth—until Lope de Vega appeared—the best playwright Spain had produced, and moreover, he was able to write (even after the public taste had been changed by Lope de Vega's plays) a kind of simple but effective style. His was a conception of the stage that was sound and avoided most of the pitfalls of Lope's new style. Lope de Vega was elegant; Cervantes was simple and logical. The modern taste has vindicated Cervantes' short plays: seen on the stage nowadays, they retain their charm and their wit. Lope de Vega's theatre is more poetic, more elegant; in many instances it is highly effective. It has impact, "it works." Yet as soon as we examine his plays with a logical mind we see that they are often artificial and implausible. Cervantes was aware of the flaws in Lope's plays and tried hard to avoid the pitfalls of the new style.

One of Cervantes' characters in *Don Quixote*, the humble but not unintelligent curate, expresses the author's reservations about the new dramatic school (Lope de Vega's, and also the vast army of Lope's followers) by bringing out "an old grudge of mine against the comedies of today, one that is equal to that which I hold against books of chivalry. For, according to Tully, a comedy should be a mirror of human life, an example of manners, and an image of the truth; yet those that we see now are mirrors of nonsense, examples of foolishness, and images of lasciviousness. In connection with the subject of which we are speaking, what could be more absurd than for a character to appear as an infant in Act I, Scene 1, and in the following scene step out as a full-bearded man? What more out of place than to depict for us an old man parading his valor, a youth who plays the cringing coward, an eloquent lackey, a page wise in giving counsel, a king turned porter, or a princess serving as a kitchen wench?"[2]

Cervantes wants his plays to be closer to reality, to everyday life, than the new fashion allows. (Let us observe, in passing, that the previous quotation is close to parody: most of Lope de Vega's plays are not as incredible as Cervantes insinuates. Moreover, Cervantes himself, in one of his short stories, *The Illustrious Kitchen Maid*, placed a noble damsel in a provincial inn as a scullery maid.)

The time element, so important to critcs of the Aristotelian school, inspires the following criticism (same character—the curate—same chapter of *Don Quixote*, I, 48): "And what shall I say of the attention that is paid to the element of time in connection with the action that is represented? I may merely tell you that I have witnessed a comedy in which the first act takes place in Europe, the second in Asia, and the third in Africa—and if there had been a fourth act, the scene would have been laid in America and thus they would have encompassed the four quarters of the globe. If fidelity to life be the principal object which a comedy should have in view, how is it possible for the most mediocre intelligence to find any satisfaction in one where the action is supposed to take place in the time of King Pepin or Charlemagne, yet which has for its leading character the Emperor Heraclius entering Jerusalem with the Holy Cross and recovering the Holy Sepulcher like Godefroi de Bouillon, when there is a vast stretch of time between the two monarchs?"[3]

II   *The First Period*

The first period of Cervantes' dramatic production ran from 1580 to 1586 or 1587. During these few years he wrote the "twenty or thirty plays" he mentions in the preface quoted above. In the Appendix to his *Voyage to Parnassus*, he mentions the titles of some of these plays: "*The Manners of Algiers, The Destruction of Numantia, The Grand Sultana, The Naval Combat, Jerusalem, Amaranta or the Mayflower, The Amorous Grove, The Rare and Matchless Arsinda,* and many others that have slipped from my memory. But that which I most esteem, and still pride myself upon, was and is one styled *The Confused Lady,* which, with peace be it spoken, may rank as good among the best of comedies of the 'Cloak and Sword' which have hitherto been represented."[4]

Most of these plays are lost to us. Only two plays belonging to this early period have been preserved: *Los tratos de Argel (The Manners of Algiers)* and his tragedy on the siege of Numantia. The first is a four-act play dealing with a sentimental and exotic subject. It tells the story of two Christian lovers, Aurelio and Silvia, who are captured by Moorish pirates and sold to Izuf and his wife Zara in Algiers. Inevitably Zara falls in love with her handsome male slave Aurelio, Izuf with pretty Silvia. The Moslem masters try to use the slaves as go-betweens without realizing that since Aurelio and Silvia love each other, they are bound to sabotage their masters' plots. The play has a happy end: the Christians are ransomed. As Richard Predmore points out, "it is not one of the author's best plays, but it is of exceptional documentary value, being full of verifiable historical incidents and plausible descriptions of life in Algiers during the late 1570's. Of special interest is a soldier named Saavedra, who acts as the firm friend and sustainer of other Christian captives. Like Velazquez in the *Maids of Honor,* Cervantes has painted his own portrait but not in the center of the canvas."[5]

The Destruction of Numantia is a more ambitious play. A tragedy in verse in the grand manner, it depicts the heroic resistance of the inhabitants of the ancient city of Numancia, a Celtiberian stronghold besieged by the Roman armies of Scipio the Younger in 134–133 B.C. The cast of characters is a large one: the protagonists are the entire population of the city. The Romans will not accept an honorable surrender. Hunger makes further resistance impossible. Every inhabitant of the city accepts death in preference to enslavement to the Romans. The men burn their homes, kill their women and children, and then commit suicide. The last one to die is a young boy, Viriato, who, bidden to surrender, hurls himself from the high wall to his death. The play ends as Fame, from atop the desolate walls of the city, proclaims the matchless heroism of its inhabitants, and announces that the unborn generations of Spaniards will be worthy of such a heritage. Although such flawless behavior is somewhat alien to modern students whose pragmatic cynicism relates them to the antiheroes of Joseph Heller's *Catch-22*, it is not hard to understand that the patriotic values exalted by Cervantes are enduring ones—the play may have inspired the inhabitants of Saragossa to heroic resistance against the Napoleonic besiegers in 1809: it was performed during the darkest hours of the city's siege. Romantic critics raved about *Numantia's* excellence: Shelley, the Schlegel brothers, Humboldt, Goethe, Sismondi, Schopenhauer, were impressed by its stark Stoic grandeur. The play is on the whole slow-moving, almost static in its pace. Yet its epic grandeur is undeniable.

III   *The Second Period*

Towards the end of his life, as we have already pointed out, Cervantes returned to the love of his youth and again became a playwright. He wrote two types of plays, *comedias* (usually long plays in verse) and *entremeses* (one-act comedies or farces, "curtain-raisers") either in verse or in prose. The short pieces are by far the best. The *comedias* often strain the credulity of the modern reader. They are very seldom performed nowadays. *El gallardo español (The Gallant Spaniard)* deals with the adventures of a Spanish soldier in North Africa. He is challenged by a Moor, leaves his camp, and goes over to the Moorish side under a false name, looking for his challenger. All sorts of romantic encounters ensue. He joins the Moors for the final attack on the Spanish camp but, at the last minute, reveals his true identity and singlehandedly saves the Spanish army. *Los baños de Argel (The Bagnios of Algiers)* is merely a series of dramatic vignettes based upon the author's remarkably persistent memories of his Algerian captivity. *La casa de los celos y selvas de Ardenia (The House of Jealousy)* is a fantastic mixture of legends. Charlemagne, Angelica, Orlando, and Bernardo del Carpio seem to dance a complicated passacaglia through half a dozen enchanted forests. *El rufián dichoso (The Happy Ruffian)* dramatizes a saint's life—a curious saint, who started life as a picaroon and a swordsman for hire. The first act, which deals with the picaresque beginnings, is by far more interesting than the mystical ending. *La gran sultana (The Grand Sultana)* is also based upon memories of his years in Algiers. The comic elements are underlined here to the limit: One would think Cervantes was writing a parody of his previous plays with the same theme. *El laberinto de* amor (Love's Labyrinth) is a confusing play that reminds us of Lope, Lohengrin, and Orlando Furioso. It deals with a young woman whose honor is attacked and who is defended by an unknown knight. The plot is almost too complicated to understand. La entretenida (The Amusing Comedy) is based on mistaken identities, two parallel couples, confusion, and mayhem. Only the end is original: the two couples do not get married after all. Pedro de Urdemalas (Peter the Artful Dodger) is a much better play. Walter Starkie calls it "the most suggestive and animated of all his plays, and so modernistic in style that it suggests the mirror theater of Pirandello."[6] Pedro, a picaroon, joins a band of gypsies out of love for a young gypsy, Belica. He has his fortune told by a seer: he will become a king, according to the seer. He becomes happy and excited: he imagines every detail of his future glory. It turns out that the seer made a mistake. It is the girl who belongs to a distinguished family of royal blood. When the truth comes out, poor Pedro is frustrated: marriage to the girl is impossible. He decides to seek a way out of his frustration: he will become an actor. After all, actors can play the role of pope, king, emperor: the road to glory is still open to him.

The best plays in this second period of Cervantes' career as a playwright are by far the eight entremeses. An entremés is a short play: one brief act to be played between the first and the second act of a longer play. These "Interludes" were usually, but not always, light, amusing, satirical. As Edwin Honig writes, "these eight short plays are among the most beguiling things Cervantes ever wrote. Part of the charm is the appropriateness of the simple dramatic form to Cervantes' lighthearted, often elusive treatment of his subjects."[7] The Interludes deal with the underworld (always a favorite subject for Cervantes) and the middle and lower classes of small towns and cities: magicians, impostors, divorce courts, country bumpkins, penniless students, talkative prostitutes. "They are brief, completely rounded-off, self-sufficient pieces, achieving a tightness of form that cannot be found in his work in the other genres. Their modesty of aim and slightness of incident are belied by the full-blooded particularity of their characters. For these are not stock types going through their paces in a well-worn anecdote, but vital individuals with distinct voices. They are dramatic in the way that Don Quixote and Sancho Panza are dramatic: their voices engage each other and depend on each other; they come alive through the irritation of their complementariness, by the mere fact that they are thrown together and must reckon with each other."[8]

Why Cervantes' Interludes are first-rate theatre is obvious. His gift was for the creation of flesh-and-blood characters and for good dialogue. In his novels, either a complex plot or the needs of the episodic narrative often tended to dilute the achievements of Cervantes' genius. A short farce was the ideal medium: it produced abrasive encounters between the characters and did not dilute the humor, charm, and wit of the dialogue.

El juez de los divorcios (The Divorce-Court Judge) is the first Interlude in the 1615 edition. It is also the shortest. The plot is almost nonexistent. Several quarreling couples air their grievances in front of a court. The judge reminds them that all marriages are like ferocious battles occasionally interrupted by brief truces.

El rufián viudo (The Pimp Who Lost His Moll), in verse, is the sad story of Trampagos, a pimp whose moll has died. In a grotesque-sentimental outburst, he enumerates for his underworld friends the virtues of the deceased. They console him and invite him to choose a new companion among the numerous available whores present at the wake.

La elección de los alcaldes de Daganzo (Choosing a Councilman in Daganzo) lampoons rustic prejudice, ignorance, and plain stupidity. The candidates in a local election turn out to be incredibly conceited and dense: yet each one defends his right to be elected. One of them can neither read nor write: so much the better, he claims, because culture always gets you in trouble with the Inquisition.

La guarda cuidadosa (The Hawk-Eyed Sentinel), in prose, is a delightful vignette in which a truculent Soldier and a smug Sacristan vie for the hand of Cristinica, a scullery maid.

El vizcaíno fingido (The Basque Impostor), also in prose, involves a trick worthy of Boccaccio's *Decameron* played by a cynical young man and his friend (who pretends to be a stupid Basque speaking broken comical Spanish) on an elegant and greedy prostitute. The trick is done with a gold chain: now you see it, now you don't.

El retablo de las maravillas (The Wonder Show) is based on an old medieval story, one that will reappear in Andersen's "The Emperor's Clothes." Chanfalla, a crooked puppeteer, plays a joke on his audience: he offers them a magic show, one that can be seen only by those who have no Jewish ancestry and are not bastards.

Everyone claims to see what is impossible to be seen—since the stage is bare: only the voice of the master of ceremonies suggests what should be seen. This sharp social satire ends in pandemonium. Social hypocrisy and prejudice are unmasked, authority is subverted.

La cueva de Salamanca (The Cave of Salamanca) is one of the best Interludes. It again reminds us of Boccaccio. Leonarda, Pancracio's wife, after complaining hypocritically about her husband's departure on a business trip, invites her lover and her servant Cristina's lover to spend the night with them. The merry party is joined by Carraolano, a student who had asked hospitality for one night. Suddenly the husband returns. The lovers hide inside two big food baskets; the student gets the mistress and her maid out of this embarrassing situation by pretending to be a magician capable of invoking a couple of devils. He warns that these devils will take the shape of two local townsmen, the sacristan and the town barber (who are in fact the two lovers). The husband is hoodwinked, the would-be adulterers go unpunished. They come out of the coal bin where they had hidden themselves at the bidding of the student, accept their roles as devils, and the husband is convinced. They all sit down to a succulent dinner. A mood of merry cynicism pervades this Interlude.

Finally, *El viejo celoso (The Jealous Old Husband)* presents a grotesque old man married to a young woman. His jealousy knows no limits. A gossipy clever woman, his neighbor, proves too smart for him: she introduces a young man, a protégé of hers, who makes love to the young wife almost under the eyes of the old man, too busy talking to the neighbor and getting incensed against everything and everybody to notice what goes on in his wife's chamber.

Several other Interludes have been attributed to Cervantes. The only one that stylistically could be his work is *Los dos habladores (The Two Great Talkers)*, a virtuoso performance for the main character, who can talk anybody to death.

What was Cervantes' secret in these highly successful Interludes? First of all, timing. The tempo is right. The surprises come at the proper moment. Timing is essential in comedy. It is the soul of farce. The situations are often outrageous, but not quite impossible. Nothing is overlooked in these short pieces. Even the characters' names have been chosen with care. As Edwin Honig puts it, "to begin with, each character fills a social role that is both typical and functional. In some instances such roles are immediately discernible in the characters' names. On the simplest level, we have the identifying noun—the Judge, the Old Man, the Porter, the Constable, and so forth. On another level, characters in their social roles are mocked by some distinguishing attribute in their names."[9] Thus, a trio of whores are called Preener, Wagtail, and Straybird. The four councilmen in Daganzo are called Cloven Hoof, Sneeze, Hardbread, and String Bean; the country bumpkins who aspire to office are identified as Gassing, Craggy, Hock, and Frog. Other characters have absurd names invented by Cervantes: Trampagos, Chiquiznaque, Chanfalla. They are meaningless—yet funny to the Spanish ear. Young wives with old or stupid husbands have realistic names such as Leonarda or Lorenza; their husbands, common names ironically distorted, like Pancracio, which according to its Greek roots may mean "all-powerful" or "all-governing," or Cañizares, which by association with dried grass or reeds suggests "straw tubes" or "hollow reeds."

Cervantes may have learned some of his tricks in the works of Plautus, the short stories of Boccaccio, the curtain-raisers by Lope de Rueda, whose plays he saw and admired as a child. Yet much is original, fresh, and typical of his genius in these short Interludes. They can still be played with success—and often are, by college theatre groups especially, in Spain and elsewhere.

CHAPTER 5

Cervantes as a Short Story Writer

I The Genre

THE *Novelas ejemplares (Exemplary Novels)* was published in 1613. The tales are closer to short story length than real full-length novels. The Spanish *novela* meant at that time "deceit," "happening, news," and finally, as a neologism, "short story." Italian writers used the word *novella* for a short prose story, *romanzo* for a full-length novel. Cervantes seems to have been the first to have used the new word, *novela,* in the title of a collection of short stories. He saw himself as a pioneer in this genre: in the prologue to his collection of short stories he declares, "To this my genius has applied itself, and this way my mind prompts me—all the more as I am now aware that I am the first to write novels in the Castilian tongue. For the many novels that circulate in print and in Spanish are all translated from foreign languages, while these are mine own, neither imitated nor stolen from anyone. My genius begat them, my pen gave them birth, and they are growing up in the arms of the printing press."[1]

It is true that Cervantes was one of the pioneers of the genre, especially if we think of the Italian *novella* as a point of departure for the modern short story. It is also true that the Spanish literature of the Middle Ages abounds in short stories of a traditional character, sometimes influenced by Oriental sources. The Italian *novella* was often mundane, witty, or sentimental. It was, more often than not, either a love story or the story of a deceit. In 1565 Antonio de Villegas had published a striking "Moorish tale," *Historia de Abindarráez y de la Hermosa Jarifa (The Story of Abindarraez and the Beautiful Jarifa).* It was a beguiling tale, both "exotic" (it took place in Spain but the characters were Moorish) and "romantic." Yet Cervantes' models were mostly the Italian writers such as Boccaccio and Bandello. Their works were popular in Spain: Boccaccio's

Decameron had been translated into Spanish under the title *Las Cien Novelas (The Hundred Short Stories)* and published in Seville in 1496; four editions of this translation were published before Boccaccio was put on the Index by the Inquisition in 1559. After that date he was no longer reprinted in Spain, although Italian copies were often smuggled into Spain by Spanish travellers. It is interesting to note that the great playwright Tirso de Molina, one of the few writers of the Golden Age to admire Cervantes' prose, was to praise warmly his short stories by calling him "our Spanish Boccaccio."

Yet Boccaccio had composed his stories in the freer atmosphere of the Italian Renaissance, at a time when the Inquisition had not yet developed its own peculiar interest in "literary criticism." The situation in Spain was vastly different, and Cervantes was aware of the increasing tensions in his country's intellectual atmosphere.

He had long been interested in the short story as a literary genre, ever since in his earliest work, *La Galatea*, he had inserted several short stories and tales which gave his pastoral romance a wealth of human situations and viewpoints. In the first part of *Don Quixote*, since he was not sure that the adventures and constant dialogue of the knight and his squire could hold the attention of his readers, he introduced tales such as "El Curioso Impertinente" ("Meddlesome Curiosity") and "La historia del Cautivo" ("The Captive's Tale") which add a touch of pathos and melodrama to the comic adventures of Don Quixote and Sancho, thus providing "tragic relief" from comedy and irony. His last novel, *Persiles y Sigismunda (Persiles and Sigismunda)*, would be a complex tapestry of interwoven tales organized around the central motif of two young lovers.

Cervantes was aware that his love of short stories might interfere in the composition of his novels. He expected that many of his readers would criticize him for introducing these tales in his novels, and felt the need to justify himself. He did so in Chapter 47 of Part I of *Don Quixote:* In works of fiction, the Canon of Toledo says, there should be a mating between the plot and the reader's intelligence. "They should be so written that the impossible is made to appear possible, things hard to believe being smoothed over and the mind held in suspense in such a manner as to create surprise and astonishment while at the same time they divert and entertain so that admiration and pleasure go hand in hand." And later on: "All of which being done in an easy-flowing style, with a skilled inventiveness that draws insofar as possible upon the truth of things, the result would surely be a web woven of beautiful and variegated threads . . ."[3] The foregoing seems to indicate that Cervantes was aware of his shortcomings in the organization of his novels: he knew that they might be reproached for lacking in unity, since so many separate tales were woven into the main story, and yet he was unable to restrain himself. His creative mind was always at work introducing new elements. Aristotelian critics and sophisticated readers were right to complain that the whole lacked unity, yet Cervantes knew that his talent for imagining new characters and new situations could not be restrained. He was a born storyteller.

He was also aware that as a short story writer and a novelist he had embarked on a perious profession. Many subjects were intrinsically dangerous. Moreover, the whole field of prose fiction was suspect. The diatribes of the moralists were a constant source of worry. As Walter Starkie puts it, "the moralists of the period were openly hostile to novels, and in Part II of *El Criticón* the Jesuit Baltasar Gracián voices the general opinion of churchmen that novels were trash, suitable for the ignorant, such as pages and laboring wenches. In the scene describing the passengers who have gone astray and are rounded up by the guards in 'Life's Custom House' and searched for contraband, one is found in possession of a book of chivalry and is roundly abused for reading such antiquated rubbish. Some of the passengers beg to be allowed to read the works of authors who had satirized such absurdities and condemned them. A symbolic character, Sanity, however, replies, denying their petition with the plea that such authors had merely tried to drive out one piece of folly and place still greater foolishness in its place. Here the writer does not mention Cervantes by name, but the barb against *Don Quixote* is implied, and he goes on to call all such novels 'useless riffraff, fit pabulum for idle ignoramuses.' "[4]

We will not be far from the mark if we assume that four factors influenced Cervantes in the writing of his "Exemplary Tales." The first and foremost force was his own creative imagination, always near the boiling point, yet in this case also always aware of the surrounding social factors. The second is the taste of his readers: No author who wants to be successful can disregard it. The third is the everpresent censorship of moralists and men of the Church: only a madman would stray far from the prescribed limits of moral taste—and Cervantes was quite sane. The fourth factor is to be found in the literary criticism of the times, on the whole conservative and dominated by Aristotelian scholars: Cervantes wanted to please them almost as much as he wanted to please his readers. The first two forces pulled him in the direction of romantic tales with overtones of fantasy and sexual misbehavior. The second group of forces pulled him in an opposite direction, towards common sense and a moralizing attitude. The *Exemplary Novels,* as much as other works of Cervantes (and, we hasten to add, of any writer in any period), are often the result of a compromise.

There is no doubt that Cervantes was aware of the moralists' criticism of fiction, no doubt also that he tried to appease them in his Preface, where, discussing his tales, he writes: "I have called them 'Exemplary,' and if you reflect on it, there is not one of them from which you may not draw a profitable example; and if I did not fear to enlarge on this subject, probably I might show you what tasty and wholesome fruit may be derived from all of them collectively as well as individually."[5]

And yet Cervantes does not want his readers to have the impression that the short stories being introduced are moral and straitlaced to the point of boredom: "My intention has been to place in the marketplace of our commonwealth a billiard table, at which everyone can entertain himself without threat to body or soul, for innocent recreation does good rather than harm."[6] (The Spanish dictionary compiled by Covarrubias, the *Tesoro* of 1621, states that the game of billiards had been introduced recently in Spain from Italy. Cervantes uses the expression *mesa de trucos,* in which the game played resembled the modern bagatelle game: it was often played at fairs, with prizes awarded the winners. Cervantes implies thus that anyone can play at the game of reading his short stories—and win.)

This is, therefore, the way in which he wants his new work to be considered: his short stories, he tells us, are both entertaining and exemplary. The avowed intent of the novels was for them to be exemplary in all respects. Yet, as J. B. Avalle-Arce points out, "not all modern critics have accepted such statements at face value, and their skepticism about such morality ranges from Ortega y Gasset's, who talked about *la hipocresía heroica* [heroic hypocrisy] of Cervantes, to Unamuno's, who wrote: *Cervantes, en sus novelas, buscó más la ejemplaridad que hoy llamaríamos estética que la moral,*

*tratando de dar con ellas horas de recreo y reposo al espíritu afligido;
las llamó ejemplares después de haberlas escrito* [In these short
stories Cervantes was more interested in what we would nowadays
call aesthetic examples than moral ones; he called them *exemplary*
after he wrote them]. But if we can argue today—and argument
there certainly is—about the correspondence between the moralizing and the actual product, insofar as the moral lesson is concerned,
there can be no such discussion about their artistic merit. For these
short novels constitute today, when one looks at them within a
historical perspective, a marvelous showcase of what the novel had
been like up to Cervantes' time, what it was like at that time, and
what it would come to be, if only one were another Cervantes."[7]

This is an important critical statement. We know that even a
pioneer has to rely on the teachings of the past. Cervantes was no exception: although he changed considerably—and in some aspects
decisively—the rules of prose fiction, he could not achieve his
breakthrough in one single moment. Much of tradition filters
through into his pages. Moreover, it is easier to see the difference
between the old and the new in a composite work, written piecemeal
during a considerable time, than by examining a unified work, such
as *Don Quixote*, written continuously. It is therefore by examining
the different parts that he assembled under the umbrella title of *Exemplary Novels* that we can begin to grasp his merit as an innovator.
These short stories offer us a spectrum of his talent, from the in-
frared of the most traditional tale to the ultraviolet of his most
original and boldest fiction. Since we are dealing, as Avalle-Arce has
pointed out, with a showcase of Cervantes' art of fiction, it becomes
imperative to deal with a thorny subject, one that has given scholars
considerable trouble: their chronological order. That is to say, we
should try to determine which was written first, which was written
after the first one, and so on. Only thus can we appreciate the evolution of Cervantes as a writer of short stories, and also, given the importance of these tales and the fact that he wrote them at the crucial
time where his literary career was reaching a climax, we can appreciate the interaction between his short stories and *Don Quixote*.
These tales could well be the crucible in which Cervantes' ideas
about literature melted into their final shape. The genre—short
story or novelette—was given to him in large part by tradition; what
he did with it was essential in determining the future of the short

story and the future of the novel. In order to appreciate it we must have a clear picture of the whole, with each part placed in succession besides the others like colors in a spectrum.

II *Chronology*

We are dealing with twelve *novellas* or "long short stories." Their order in the first edition tells us nothing about their dates of composition: we assume the publisher, or Cervantes himself, arranged them in that sequence just to introduce greater variety and please the readers. The printed sequence is as follows: *La gitanilla (The Little Gypsy), El amante liberal (The Generous Lover), Rinconete y Cortadillo (Rinconete and Cortadillo), La española inglesa (The Spanish Englishwoman), El Licenciado Vidriera (The Man of Glass, or The Glass Scholar), La fuerza de la sangre (The Power of Blood), El celoso extremeño (The Jealous Extremaduran), La ilustre fregona (The Illustrious Kitchen Maid), Las dos doncellas (The Two Maidens), La Señora Cornelia (Mrs. Cornelia), El casamiento engañoso (The Deceitful Marriage)* and *El coloquio de los perros (The Dogs' Colloquy).*

The task of determining the sequence of these twelve novels has occupied many scholars for a long time without any definite conclusions having ever been attained. Only a few definite facts exist. We know, for instance, that in order to amuse the Cardinal Niño de Guevara during his long summer vacations, his assistant Francisco Porras de la Cámara gathered together different texts of various kinds—fabulous adventures, merry tales, curious letters, proverbs, tales of adventures, etc.—in a compendium which he entitled *Compilación de curiosidades españolas (Anthology of Spanish Curiosities)* and in this compilation were included two unpublished manuscripts by Cervantes, *Rinconete y Cortadillo* and *El celoso extremeño*. These two tales were later included by Cervantes in his *Exemplary Novels*—not without several significant changes in the text. The exact date of this anthology is not known, but we assume with good reason that it must have been 1604.

These two short stories are therefore probably older than *Don Quixote*. Probably older than *Don Quixote* are also the tale *Meddlesome Curiosity* and *The Captive's Tale*, which Cervantes inserted in his novel. Perhaps *The Spanish Englishwoman* is also a novel belonging to this early period. *The Deceitful Marriage* and

The Dog's Colloquy must have been composed during Cervantes' stay in Valladolid (1604–1606) and *The Illustrious Kitchen Maid* and *The Little Gypsy* were probably written during his years in Madrid which followed immediately afterwards. This is all conjecture—although logical and well founded.

Little is known about the composition of the other short stories. Perhaps an attempt at classification will help. The great diversity of these short stories has prompted Cervantes' critics to attempt a classification of these works along different lines. Among the most interesting is the classification by Rodríguez Marín, who distinguished between a group of stories that are wholly or partly autobiographical, another group that was the product of Cervantes' imagination, and a third group in which Cervantes imitates Italian stories, although certain details in them are to be attributed to his own experiences.

A great Spanish contemporary critic, Dámaso Alonso, remarks that in the *Exemplary Novels* Cervantes' polarization between idealism and realism crystallized in narrations which are excessively idealized, if we take into account a division or classification which would set aside the "idealistic" novels on one hand and the "realistic novels" on the other. The first tales depict characters who are unifaceted and therefore false, who combine in themselves every conceivable moral beauty—and frequently also physical beauty. We may find such a hero, for example, in Ricardo, the protagonist of *The Generous Lover*, who is the epitome of goodness and generosity, just as his beloved Leonisa is the incarnation of human beauty. Equally beautiful and good to an exceptional degree is Isabela, the "Spanish Englishwoman," who is carried to England after the attack on Cadiz, and no less extraordinary is the young Englishman Recaredo, who continues loving her even after poison has disfigured her face. Dámaso Alonso points out that "in general [the idealized novels] give us a skimpy picture of everyday reality, or else they give us details that are determined by canons of abstract beauty, while the tales that portray picaresque customs are often full of local color and everyday realistic details in the description of character types, in the way people speak, in ordinary things and the environment."[8]

Two poles, therefore: idealization and the picaresque. The most attractive tales to the modern reader are the novels that are alike in these respects: they have no love plot, or if they do have one, it is unimportant and contains no romantic idealizations; the tale lacks a central unifying thread or, in other words, a visible plot, and consists mainly in a succession of scenes without a clear beginning or an end, without an attempt to reach a climax; these are, therefore, novels which are "porous," open, without a dramatic final scene, without an obvious scaffolding or structure. They are made up of anecdotes, of wanderings, of fleeting impressions, which, however, give birth to powerful intuitions about individual characters and even about collective life. Finally, people and objects are described in these stories with precise and abundant details until the reader thinks he can almost touch them. Of such a nature are *Rinconete and Cortadillo, The Deceitful Marriage,* and *The Dogs' Colloquy.* It is in these tales that Cervantes' art as a storyteller reaches its climax. It is interesting to notice that no moral example can be drawn from these short masterpieces—at least no moral norm that Cervantes' society could accept readily.

We come therefore, reluctantly, to a strange and confusing conclusion: according to the facts available to us, some of the best—most realistic, most original—tales in the collection belong to an early period, some of the tales that seem to our modern taste weaker and more derivative may have been written in later years, after *Don Quixote* (Part I), and this would indicate not an evolution in the art of Cervantes, but rather an involution, a retrogression. How is this to be explained?

How could a writer who had created the lively characters of *Rinconete and Cortadillo* and the bold social criticism of *The Jealous Extremaduran* accept later on all the conventions and literary fashions of his time? Didn't Cervantes realize how innovative and creative his new approach to the art of the short story had been?

This enigma cannot be completely solved until and unless a clear chronology of his stories can be established. Perhaps some day a manuscript with dates will be discovered. Perhaps the patient efforts of many scholars will in the future produce conclusions that are clear and precise. For the moment we are left with two alternatives. The first is to believe that the best stories were written after the weaker ones, that these weaker stories had been composed several years before *Don Quixote* and left in a drawer, and that finally, the success of his novel compelled Cervantes to prepare a new work in which he added some stories to the old ones, the new ones being the stories we now perceive to be his best work.

This theory is on shaky grounds. All the evidence points to the priority of *Rinconete and Cortadillo, The Jealous Extremaduran,* and *The Little Gypsy,* also one of his best novels. It is also absurd to think that he was unaware of the quality of his work. He was, on the contrary, extremely proud of what he had written: "My genius begat them, my pen gave them birth, and they are growing up in the arms of the printing press," he claims in his Preface. Walter Starkie comments: "Few more arrogant literary declarations have ever been made by a writer introducing his own works to the public. Such arrogance should be forgiven in an author who had learned by bitter experience to measure the hostility of his enemies at the moment when he awaited the publication of his volume, which would be exposed to all the vicissitudes of literary criticism. Yet, with the prescience of genius, he seemed to foresee the day, one hundred and seventy years later, when Goethe would discover in him a fellow genius, and in the *Exemplary Novels* a masterwork containing the permanent essentials of literary art. Still later, Walter Scott claimed him as the storyteller who had inspired him to become a writer."[9]

The second alternative is that Cervantes thought that his reading public was not ready for his new brand of art. The Italianate novel was still very much in fashion. Why not write a few more short stories according to the taste of the day? There was no harm in it. His "easy" stories would thus help the "difficult" ones, i.e., the stories without a clear plot, without too much sentimentality, to be accepted. Moreover, we know that after the publication of the first part of *Don Quixote* Cervantes had become famous; the straitlaced moralists and censors were sure to take notice of his new work. Precautions must be taken. Thus, the published version of *The Jealous Extremaduran* softpedals the risqué passages of the first manuscript. In the Porras anthology, adultery takes place; in the version printed in 1613, the would-be lovers, after a vain attempt at seduction on the part of the young man, fall asleep in each other's arms—without any further attempt on the part of the frustrated Don Juan.

Let us now examine these stories one by one.

III   The Little Gypsy

This is the first short story in the published edition. In it Cervantes rescues the world of gypsies from literary limbo and treats it with a respect verging on idealization. Here is the plot: A young gentleman, Juan de Cárcamo, falls in love with a young gypsy maiden, Preciosa, as beautiful as she is virtuous, born to be, as an old gypsy says, "the flower and essence of all beauty," who belongs to a troupe of wandering gypsies and dances at their performances. Preciosa demands that Cárcamo, in order to be worthy of her love, abandon his family and become a member of her tribe. He accepts and begins to live like a gypsy until, when accused of a robbery, his identity is revealed. It is then learned that neither is Preciosa a true gypsy by birth, but rather the daughter of a magistrate *(Corregidor):* She had been kidnapped as a child by an old gypsy woman. The novel ends with the marriage of the lovers. Coincidences and a happy end play an important part in the story, but what the modern reader prefers is the portrait of gypsy life with its freedom and its ancient lore. Preciosa is only fifteen years old, but as wise as she is beautiful. "Our mind," she says, "is different from yours; our understanding makes us older than our years. We sail over strange seas, and plot our course by a polestar that is unknown to you, and you will never find a foolish gypsy man or a simple gypsy woman. In truth there is no gypsy girl of twelve who does not know more than a Spanish lady of twenty-five."[10]

A contemporary Spanish critic, Juan Luis Alborg, points out that "there has been no lack of critics who thought that Cervantes did not have the same intimate knowledge of gypsy life that he possessed with respect to the rogues portrayed in *Rinconete and Cortadillo.* They base this assumption, among other reasons, on the absence of the gypsy dialect in this work. This reason does not seem entirely valid. For Cervantes may have thought that this difficult language, which was not paramount to his objective, would only make the novel heavy and hard to understand. With respect to the excessively pleasant and optimistic vision of gypsy life, this can be explained in that for the author gypsies were only picturesque outsiders in Spanish national life—in spite of the problems that they created—and were not a part of the basic social fabric, against which it would have been worth while to aim his satire, as he did so effectively in many other places."[11]

Cervantes, who for many years had led a wandering life, sympathized with the gypsies. It is not clear how well he knew them, but certainly he seems to have been more familiar with their customs and psychology than any other Spanish writer of his age. In any case, Cervantes' tale is not a sociological book, but rather a joyous celebration of the freedom that comes from a wandering life and of Preciosa's beauty. His female leading character has haunted writers of succeeding ages: she reappears in Goethe's Mignon, in Pushkins's *The Gypsies*, in Victor Hugo's Esmeralda (in *Notre Dame de Paris*), as well as in a modern ballad by Federico García Lorca, *Preciosa y el aire (Preciosa and the Wind)*.

As the contemporary Spanish critic Joaquín Casalduero has pointed out, this short story was composed with aesthetic goals in mind, not with the object of portraying faithfully reality or a social milieu. There is a rhythm of song and dance: Preciosa dances and sings in an exceptional manner and we can almost hear the music she dances to. Preciosa is a poetic being, a female Ariel who turns everything she touches into grace and poetry. Her travels constitute a strange adventure, yet there is nothing absurd or impossible in what she does or says. She is exceptional, yet she is not an artificial or impossible being: her grace and agility are always down-to-earth. To sum up: this long short story has always been a favorite among Cervantes' readers; there is a touch of magic in it, yet we are never far away from daily life.

IV   The Generous Lover

This story follows after *The Little Gypsy* in the published text. Many scholars think it was written early. In any case, it is one of the weakest and least interesting of the book. Its theme relates it to some of Cervantes' comedies dealing with prison life. Many details seem to come from Cervantes' experiences as a soldier and his capitivity in North Africa, although the action does not take place in Africa but in Turkey, and the protagonists are not Spaniards but Sicilians. It is clearly a story influenced by the "Italian Style." It deals with the voyages of two young lovers, Ricardo and Leonisa, who wander off into the Eastern Mediterranean and are taken prisoner by the Turks. They manage to ward off all the amorous advances to which they are subject during their capitivity, and finally regain their freedom and "live happily ever after." The male hero is too romantic and perfect to be credible. Some of the adventures are also hard to believe. The best feature is the description of sea travel.

V   Rinconete and Cortadillo

This is, many believe, one of the best short stories ever written by Cervantes. To read it after *The Generous Lover* can be compared to the experience of reading a good short story in the magazine *The New Yorker* after reading an old-fashioned story by a second-rate imitator of O. Henry. As J. L. Alborg states, "even if Cervantes had not written *Don Quixote,* he would have a place of honor in Spanish literature simply as the author of *Rinconete and Cortadillo.* Furthermore, while recognizing the hazards in any absolute judgment, we would dare to maintain that after *Don Quixote* this novel is the most outstanding work of its kind that has even been written in Spanish."[12]

It is difficult to give a résumé of its plot since there is really no plot, not in any traditional sense of the term. It is rather a picturesque frieze or fresco, a succession of vignettes populated by human types that represent every aspect of the underworld of Seville. We meet at the very outset two young boys, two "apprentice rogues" who have left their homes and are wandering towards Seville in search of fortune and adventures. Within a short time they come in contact with a union of rogues: it is made up of ruffians, assassins for hire, beggars, prostitutes, and other riffraff. They are all perfectly organized under the leadership of a formidable character whose name is Monipodio. This gang has all the characteristics of an institution, following rules and bylaws: one can say that it has industrialized delinquency and has managed to stabilize its relationships with society and the police. Since they work as a group and always help each other, they have achieved a remarkable efficiency. The warm sense of brotherhood, of goals shared, of dangers to be surmounted by sticking together, permeates each act of this gang. They know how to elude the pressures of the police—that is, when they are not cooperating with it by corrupting it and offering the policemen a share of the business, "a piece of the action." In order not to leave anything to chance, they even have their heavenly patrons, their favorite saints to whom they offer gifts and masses, like any other honorable institution. They want to be on good terms with everybody, and succeed most of the time.

This picture is remarkable for its mixture of cynicism and realism, the precision in the details of its setting, the ease and charm of the dialogue, the psychological truth in the situations described. These rogues can be witty; they are smart and alert, and above all, they know how to enjoy humor. This picture of local color slowly becomes a picture of implacable satire of all the "upper classes," all the so-called respectable people who not only made possible the activity of the underworld, but also seemed to tolerate it and made it prosper because they themselves were busy in parallel efforts to cheat and rob their fellowmen.

It has always been said that a writer who wants to succeed must write about an environment he knows well. Cervantes' knowledge of the milieu he describes is precise and rings true: he was obviously well acquainted with the underworld, whether because of his long stay in Seville, a city that was almost completely in the hands of the underworld, or due to his experiences in jail. Seville was at that time a fascinating city. It was wealthy and corrupt. It offered a variety of experiences and of human types not to be found in any other Spanish city. A writer gifted with sensitivity and the capacity for accurate observation—and curious about every angle of human life—such as Cervantes, was to find in Seville all the lessons that he could not have found in Salamanca, the Sorbonne, Oxford, or Cambridge. His long residence in Seville, the kind of people whom he met because of his occupation and his social position, and even his frequent jail sentences, allowed him to acquire first-hand experience with Spain's gangsters, with their customs, and their dialect. The fact that the novel—or, if we wish, the long short story—was still a virgin field where any writer could dictate the rules of the game allowed him to develop his characters: the stage was still too rigid for such fluid material, his genius too restless to limit the development and the descriptions that make up this novelette.

The conversation of rogues, as reported by Cervantes, is an intriguing mixture of conventional piety and cynicism. They do not see themselves as outsiders, but rather as intelligent members of society, able to earn their living without hard effort and always keeping open the channels of communication to the Heavenly powers. One of them explains thus their behavior to young Cortadillo: "We say our rosary at intervals during all the days of the week, and many of us don't steal on Friday or hold converse with any woman named Mary on Saturdays." The young man replies: "All this . . . fills me with admiration, but I wonder if your worship could tell me whether you have any penance to perform. Does any restitution have to be made?" The rogue replies, "As for restitution, don't mention the word. That is an impossibility, owing to the many parts into which a theft has to be divided before each agent and contractor has received its share. And so the original thief would find it impossible to make restitution, especially since there is no one to compel us to do anything of the kind, seeing that we never go to confession, and if letters of excommunication are launched against us, they never come to our notice, for we avoid the church on the days where they are read out and go there only when there is a Jubilee, so that we can reap a rich harvest from the crowds of people who gather there." Cortadillo presses on: "If this is all these gentlemen do, how can they say that their lives are good and holy?" The answer: "Why not? What is bad? Is it not worse to be a heretic or a renegade, or to kill your father, or mother, or be a Solomite?" "Your worship must mean Sodomite." "I mean that."[13]

We are of course used to literary explorations of the underground: they are commonplace in contemporary literature. It was new ground for Cervantes to cover, and it would be difficult to find a parallel to these pages outside the Spanish picaresque literature of the period.

In view of its background and its protagonists, it is clear that *Rinconete and Cortadillo* belongs, at least in principle, to the world of the picaresque novel. And yet Cervantes, who borrowed so much from all the literary genres of his period, always surpassed and changed them in his creative process. His short story differs from the usual picaresque novel in certain formal aspects, in what we may call its technique; Cervantes' rogues do not relate their own adventures in the first person singular, as is the custom in all the picaresque novels. More important, Cervantes' tale lacks the bitterness, the pessimism of most of these novels. It also lacks the moralizing tone of many of these tales. The picaresque novel developed independently from Cervantes. It was born somewhat earlier and followed a different path. Cervantes never imitated it slavishly or even clearly, not even in *Rinconete and Cortadillo*, which deals with more or less the same environment that the picaresque novels describe. We do not find in Cervantes' tale the deep psychology of marginal men that *Guzmán de Alfarache* exposes. Cervantes' goal points towards an intense gaiety, a luminous enjoyment, a sort of artistic indulgence in the forbidden fruit, which makes us forget the ugly and criminal aspects of the lives he describes.

Damon Runyon, the great teller of tales of American gangsters, could approve of Cervantes' characters. Cervantes looks at the underworld with the eyes of a poet. His style is therefore very different from the style of the true picaresque writers. It is fluid and whimsical, while the style of *Lazarillo de Tormes*, for instance, the typical picaresque novel according to some critics, and according to others the forerunner of all picaresque novels, is sober and spare, and the style of Mateo Alemán, the celebrated writer of *Guzmán de Alfarache*, is dry, witty, bitter. It is therefore an illusion for us to think that Cervantes invaded the field of picaresque literature: we can observe that Rinconete and Cortadillo, his two would-be rogues, are not the victims but the agents of the action. In the picaresque novels, we are always confronted with a desperate hero in search of survival. As a contemporary Spanish critic, Carlos Blanco Aguinaga, has pointed out, we should recall that two of the main traits of the picaresque novel are, first, that we usually deal with the story of a vagabond without any means of fortune who has to find any means to survive: hunger is therefore the antihero's first and foremost motivation. in order to satisfy his hunger with the least possible work, the picaroon will do anything he can—commit any crime, betray his friends, debase himself—without in the meantime achieving any other goal. He manages to survive, and this is the only aim that counts for him. He serves several masters; he begs, steals and dupes. The world, as seen from his limited viewpoint, seems to have no higher existential goal than his own. Cynicism pervades his every thought. When some characters do seem to aim for higher goals, we are immediately warned by the author—or by the picaroon who is his mouthpiece—that it is all vanity, empty gesturing.

Compared with the heroes of early fiction, especially with the dashing knights of the chivalry romances, and also with some of Cervantes' heroes in his short stories, the picaroon is of course an antihero. He may be lowly, but he is everpresent: the second trait mentioned by Blanco Aguinaga (and one that we have mentioned before) is that the adventures of the picaroon are always narrated in autobiographical form.

As Blanco Aguinaga sees it, "from the fusion of these two traits we may derive a third in which substance and form are quite the same:

the picaroon is always a lone wanderer, a true exile who never achieves authentic dialogue with other men because most of them distrust him and he distrusts them all, once he has acquired a little experience."[14] As the story develops, we begin to realize that every aspect of "reality" is conveyed to us through the single lens of the picaroon: he is the one who digests for us both his own adventures and the events that befall other characters; he is lonely and bitter, and so is the view of the world that we are allowed to see in his descriptions; the loneliness of the picaroon results in a sort of total isolation from the outside world. Therefore, it avoids outside judgment and justifies itself: it is precisely because he is lonely and desperate that he can afford to judge and condemn everyone else. How could they understand him and share his experiences? He can at least see them from the outside—and his bitterness filters into every aspect of other peoples' lives, contaminates every idealization, every moral principle. Reality becomes distorted, perhaps, and yet the reader begins to suspect that this is the way the world was shaped from the very beginning: the picaroon is unhappy not only because he is lonely and despised, but also because in a humble way he is part of a world that is evil, humble, and to be despised.

Rinconete and Cortadillo differs from the picaresque, as we have pointed out, in the fact that it is a tale that seems to open up to an undetermined future: there is no strict chain that links its antiheroes to a specific place and makes them move to and fro like puppets suspended from a string. Its very beginning seems to be an accident, something that happened by mere chance—and perhaps would not have happened if circumstances had been slightly different: "At the inn of Molinillo, which lies on the famous plain of Alcudia as we travel from Castile to Andalusia, on a hot summer day two boys of perhaps fourteen or fifteen met by chance . . ."[15] This is the beginning of a story in which most of what happens will be revealed through dialogue, the dialogue of the two boys, and also their conversations with the rogues in Seville: yet there is nothing that can be absolutely pinned down, clearly and scientifically defined, in a dialogue that is usually full of feints and clever wordplay. No aspect of the present will propel the two would-be rogues into the future against their will: just as Don Quixote let himself be guided by Rocinante, so they are going to let themselves be guided by chance, luck, destiny.

The two boys hesitate at first to speak the truth to each other, yet finally they tell each other their names and discuss their families. Afterward they join forces, deceive the muleteer, rob the travellers that are taking them to Seville, and end up in the courtyard of Monipodio, the king of local gangsters. What happens then is almost a tale within the tale: the two boys observe what goes on without passing any moral judgment; as the tale unfolds our admiration for the rogues of Seville grows, and so does the wonder and admiration of the two lads, and yet they seem to come to the conclusion that the game is too dangerous for them. They are not ready for it, and Rinconete, who seems to be the moralist in this strange duo, or perhaps is the more timid and prudent of the two boys, argues that it is time to go elsewhere and find less dangerous ways to earn a living. Yet the end is left wide open: "But in spite of all this, led by his youth and inexperience, he went on with this life for several months, during which occurred things that call for lengthier exposition, and so it is left for another occasion to recount his life and miracles, along with those of his master Monipodio . . ." [16] The future can be only guessed at—we see it through a glass, darklym Once more human freedom is depicted as fluid: it cannot be pinned down, the reader remains with the hope of more adventures, more life, endless possibilities.

Cervantes introduces an element of uncertainty from the very beginning: a chance encounter can lead us towards a number of paths, no conclusion is unavoidable. The European novel of the following centuries will take a cue from such uncertain a framework. The environment is to be taken into account, it can explain much; yet it should not overwhelm the characters, for where there is no freedom there can be no spontaneity, no surprise for the reader—or for the characters. The idea that the characters of a novel can have an autonomous being, that they should be as independent as possible from their creator, was bound to play a basic role in the development of the modern novel. There is only a limited number of novels, some of them undoubtedly good ones, in which human freedom is stifled: the novels created by Zola and his followers in which the extreme Naturalistic theories come into full bloom. In these works it is the background that decides every development: from the very beginning the characters are slaves to their social and economic milieu, to their biological heredity. Therefore we are right in seeing in these novels an offshoot of the Spanish picaresque literature. Zola and Mateo Alemán are guided by high moral principles: art must be placed at the service of social criticism, literature should become the handmaiden of politics. Soviet social realism is basically not too different from this trend. Cervantes would have disagreed: he was not averse to criticizing the Establishment, but he thought that art had a destiny of its own. Social criticism was a welcome by-product of the work of art, not its main ingredient or its major goal.

Dogmatic distortions have no place in Cervantes' version of picaresque realism. Moralizing was not his favorite role. Perhaps Carlos Blanco Aguinaga is the critic who has come closest to the definition of Cervantes as a novelist when he states: "Writing novels for Cervantes is, in some sense, letting do and letting live in the created world of half-truths and half-lies which no one has yet known how to demarcate satisfactorily. This is a vision of the world that tells us that the novelist (a most rare inventor) is indeed like a god who by the word casts forth reality, though like a god perhaps a bit skeptical of his ability to judge, however confident of the freedom of his creation and full of love for it."[17]

To put it succinctly, Cervantes at his best—in a tale like *Rinconete and Cortadillo,* and also in *Don Quixote*—is opposed to the facile Manichean division between "the good guys" and "the bad guys." His picture of reality is complex and ambiguous: he involves the reader in this conception. He avoids absolute moral judgments because he does not think they are possible or desirable—especially in literature. What he gives us is a multifaceted presentation of lives coming into being, struggling to become: in this sense he can be called an Existentialist writer.

VI The Spanish Englishwoman

To read this story after *Rinconete and Cortadillo* is to feel disappointed. Cervantes falls back on the tricks of the Italian school of short story writers. This tale is a curious mixture: on the one hand, romantic adventures, strange coincidences, the usual tricks; on the other, old personal memories of the author.

This is the plot: In one of the sackings of the city of Cadiz by the English, an English warrior captures and brings to England a six-year-old girl, Isabela. She is brought up by the Englishman and his wife, who are Catholic. After a period of time, the son of the warrior, Ricaredo, falls in love with Isabela and asks her hand in marriage.

Queen Elizabeth agrees to the betrothal of the young couple. But to
make Ricaredo worthy of Isabela as a bride, the Queen demands of
him a feat of great daring. She makes him captain of a
privateer—which entails for Ricaredo a crisis of conscience. He is
secretly a Catholic (like his parents). In this position he will have to
fight against Catholics—or if he fails to do so, either his secret will
be out or he will be considered a coward, and in neither case will he
win the prize of Isabela's hand.

On the high seas his fellow captain appointed by the Queen dies
and he assumes full command. He encounters two Turkish galleys
that are towing a captured Portuguese ship. He attacks them and
conquers them. The Portuguese ship was returning from the Indies
with a precious cargo which Ricaredo seizes. He frees the prisoners,
most of whom are Spanish Catholics. An old couple, who turn out to
be the parents of Isabela, beg him to take them to England, where
the ships and their crew make a triumphal entrance. Parents and
daughter recognize each other, and the Queen agrees to the
marriage of the lovers.

The plot develops further into what we might call "Golden Age
Soap Opera." It turns out that "the arrogant and haughty Count
Arnesto," son of the first lady-in-waiting to the Queen, has fallen in
love with Isabela and now demands that his mother request her
hand from the Queen. The Queen, however, keeps her word, and
the Count challenges Ricaredo to a duel but is made prisoner by the
royal guard, and his desperate mother then poisons the girl, who is
saved from death only after losing her beauty. In spite of her
present ugliness Ricaredo wishes to proceed with the marriage, but
his parents arrange for a new marriage for their son with a Scottish
heiress. Isabela and her parents leave for Spain after Ricaredo has
promised Isabela that he will join her within two years. In Spain,
Isabela slowly recovers her health and also her extraordinary beauty.
Confusing rumors of Ricaredo's death arrive; Isabela, disconsolate,
takes to a convent. But Ricaredo, who had fallen into the hands of
pirates but managed to escape, appears, and the couple are finally
married.

Critics have often observed one particular aspect about this tale:
the generous way in which Cervantes treats the Queen of England,
which was contrary to the opinion held by most Spaniards of his
time. There was a general distaste for Elizabeth, nourished by a dou-

ble hostility, political and religious. Perhaps it was only chivalry on the part of Cervantes.

VII   The Man of Glass

This is one of the most original and strangest of Cervantes' novelettes. The plot is almost nonexistent. The hero is a madman. It has, therefore, a particular fascination for the admirers of *Don Quixote:* A young man, the Licentiate Tomás Rodaja, becomes convinced that he is made of glass, and therefore he is in perpetual fear of being broken. He is, in a way, the "younger brother" of Don Quixote. Did Cervantes create his glass hero simultaneously with his famous knight? Was his fragile hero an afterthought, a by-product of Cervantes' major novel? Should we assume that Cervantes created his Man of Glass before he gave birth to Don Quixote? These questions cannot be answered for the moment. Suffice it to say that we are dealing here with a satirical tale—and that satire is the special province chosen by Cervantes for his art.

Was there a real-life model for Cervantes' glass hero? A Spanish scholar, S. Rivera Manescan, claims that this was possibly the case.[18] Cervantes was probably acquainted with Don Alonso de Santa Cruz, a physician at the court of Philip II, who wrote a treatise on melancholy—at that time considered in its extreme forms a sort of madness. This book was published after Cervantes' death, but its author could have discussed parts of its contents with Cervantes much before its publication. Both men lived in Valladolid in the years 1604—1606 and may have discussed madness and its different forms, a subject of interest for both of them. Dr. Santa Cruz describes in his book the strange case of one of the patients of his professor of medicine at the Sorbonne in Paris, a man who was firmly convinced that he was made of glass and was afraid to be touched by his friends lest he be broken. In any case, Cervantes' madman acquires a new dimension. He is not only a madman: he is also an intellectual—and a seer. He changes his personality in the course of his development. He begins by being Tomás Rodaja, a poor fellow who studies law in Salamanca and is helped out of pity by two fellow students of the upper classes. Along with his protectors he attends the University where he distinguishes himself by his intelligence and his love for science.

Moved by the spirit of adventure, he leaves his studies and enrolls in the Army. He goes to Italy and lives for a while in that country which for the Spaniards of his time seemed to be a Paradise on earth. Returning to Salamanca to go on with his studies, he falls prey to a scheming woman who, in order to bend his will, gives him a love potion. After a long delirium between life and death, he is left with a strange insanity: he believes he is made of glass and thus must avoid any contact with his fellowmen out of fear that his body will be shattered to pieces. Because of this strange obsession, he is called The Glass Scholar and people seek out his company in order to enjoy his witty sayings and the way he discusses any topic proposed by his audience. As the French critic Foulché-Delbosc has remarked, he suffers from the most generous form of madness in the world: the madness for truth. He may be, in fact, the mouthpiece for the personality of Cervantes himself, and according to Schlegel, none of the other short stories, not even the stories inserted in *Don Quixote,* sheds more light on the soul of Cervantes or conveys better his judgments on human society.

Finally cured, thanks to the cares of a priest, he gets ready to work as a lawyer and plead a case before a tribunal. But at the time of his recovery the paradox appears: the very men who thought him interesting as a madman prove indifferent when confronted with his normalcy. And Tomás Rodaja, once more obliged to earn a daily living, enlists again in the Army and is shipped out to Flanders. As the critic J. B. Avalle-Arce puts it, "forced by circumstances, he ceases to be a spectator of life and stops criticizing life to plunge into it. It is at this moment that his life acquires full meaning: his name is no longer the diminutive form (Rodaja), nor an alias (Vidriera); it is the positive, full form Rueda. But this period is the briefest of them all and ends abruptly, with Rueda killed by that very life of action he had chosen. In it, however, he has found his salvation and will survive death, for, as Cervantes writes at the end of the story, '(Tomás Rueda died) winning at his death the reputation of a wise man and a most valiant soldier.' "[19]

The hero's life is divided into three parts, each one symbolized by one of his names. Each part of his life entails a rebirth and therefore a new name is called for. The name "Vidriera" (glass, glass window) is most appropriate to his period as a critic and "seer": he helps us see through things and people. He is a spectator and a critic. In this stage all action is stopped, all the biographic pretense comes to an end: we are facing a man who is not himself. He is both a seer, a madman, and simply a piece of glass through which we can see the truth about things, society, history. He is wise enough about himself: "I have not been so foolish as to become a bad poet, nor so fortunate as to deserve to be a good one." His wisdom can easily be accepted and put to good use. When someone asks him what he should do in order not to envy anyone, he replies: "Sleep, for all the time you are dozing you will be the equal of the man you envy." His wisdom is a mixture of common sense and absurdities: it is on the whole startling. It is often bitterly satirical. Only a madman could afford to be so outspoken. Several critics have come to the conclusion that the novelette was only a pretext, an excuse, that would make it plausible for Cervantes (or rather his mouthpiece, the Man of Glass) to spin out a long list of critical sentences. The tale makes plain what any reader of *Don Quixote* has suspected: Cervantes is especially fond of madmen, perhaps because madmen—and also children—are capable of telling the rest of the world the unpleasant truths nobody wants to hear.

Cervantes' tale is interesting and on the whole original: yet we hesitate to call it completely successful. The madman's glimpses of wisdom shoot off in all directions without focusing upon one meaningful center. He becomes a puppet without a clear goal. A paradox hovers over the tale: when healed, the Glass Man can find no audience, becomes unemployed. The end—military glory—is also an anticlimax. He goes off to war, dies in Flanders, the Vietnam of Spain in the Golden Age. What did temporary wisdom do for him? We are left with a bitter feeling.

VIII   The Power of Blood

Perhaps the only description that fits this novelette is "Italianate Absurd Melodrama." A young girl, Leocadia, is kidnapped and seduced—raped is perhaps the apt word—by an unknown young man who leaves for Italy shortly afterwards. A child is born. After a while the child is wounded in an accident: by chance it is the child's paternal grandfather who comes to his rescue and takes him home. The child's mother, Leocadia, comes to the house where her child is being cared for; she recognizes the very room where she was seduced; she tells her sad story to the parents of her seducer. They compel their son to come back from Italy.

The end is not hard to guess. He is still in love with the girl he seduced. He marries her. The future looks bright for the young couple. She has forgiven him. They kiss. The background music increases. Fade out.

Obviously the psychology of this tale's characters leaves much to be desired. The reaction of the seduced girl is implausible. She is too ready to forgive. The parents are also not quite believable. The happy ending is artificial. Cervantes had so many excellent tales to his credit that he thought he could afford this "bomb." His critics seem to agree: on the whole they seem to take leave of their critical sense when their favorite author does the same.

IX   The Jealous Extremaduran

This tale is a minor masterpiece. The plot is not too complicated. A rich old man, Felipe de Carrizales, returns from America and marries a very young girl of great beauty. His senile passion turns to jealousy. He locks up his wife in the house. He has the windows boarded up. No one is allowed into the house.

The very abundance of precautions calls attention to the house and its obsessed master. A young man, idle and depraved, whose name is Loaysa, finds out about the old man and his young bride, and decides to seduce her. He manages to talk the duenna and the servants into letting him in at night. The old man is put to sleep with the help of a powerful drug. In the original draft the seducer has his way with the girl; the second version is somewhat bowdlerized (and less believable) and leaves the wife's honor intact. In both versions, the old man wakes up in the morning and finds the couple in bed. His grief overwhelms him to the point that he is incapable of taking revenge. He dies soon afterward, not without first forgiving the guilty couple. He even advises his wife to marry Loaysa after his death. However, she is overcome by remorse and enters a convent. The best pages in this novelette deal with the psychological motivation of the characters, with their changes in mood, and especially with the vicarious excitement of the servants who seem to derive a perversed pleasure from the thought that their mistress is about to be seduced.

X   The Illustrious Kitchen Maid

This romantic tale is not altogether believable and yet it has charm and several excellent descriptions dealing with life in the city of Toledo. The tale narrates the adventures and misadventures of two sons of noble families who have become picaroons out of love for adventure. These nobles disguised as picaroons allow us to glimpse "real life." Don Diego de Carriazo and his friend Tomás de Avendaño arrive at Toledo and are lodged in an inn where one of them falls in love with a beautiful scullery maid. She is actually the daughter of a noble family, but the young man does not know it yet. He decides to stay as a servant so as to be near her. The most interesting pages describe the life of the lower classes in the city, the dances, the serenades, fishing in nearby lakes. The plot is almost incredible and too sentimental, but the descriptions are first-rate. At the end the girl reveals her noble origin and the couple are happily married.

XI   The Two Maidens

One of the weakest novelettes in this collection, the plot is almost unbelievable. Two girls dressed as men—a device that was popular in the theatre and the novels of that time—seek out the seducer of one of them. After many and complicated adventures, they run into him in Barcelona, and the story ends with a double wedding since the brother of the injured girl marries her friend. Not even the most ardent Cervantists have much good to say about this tale.

XII   Mrs. Cornelia

An optimistic and excessively "rosy" novel, the action takes place in the Italian city of Bologna. The protagonists are two Spanish gentlemen, D. Antonio de Isunza and D. Juan de Gamboa. On the same night two very different things happen to them: D. Antonio is spoken to from a dark portico, and a bundle is delivered to him—which turns out to be a newly-born infant. D. Juan is asked to succor a veiled lady. All turn up later at the same inn where the mystery is happily resolved: the veiled woman is Cornelia, a great beauty, and the child is her son, the fruit of her union with the Duke of Ferrara, who had promised to marry her. They all go to seek out the Duke, and finally the wedding takes place.

XIII   The Deceitful Marriage *and* The Dogs' Colloquy

As J. B. Avalle-Arce indicates, these two novels present a structural problem. They are two separate novels, "but they are so inextricably interrelated that they are really one. Cervantes tells us that he wrote twelve *Novelas ejemplares,* which probably means that, *a posteriori,* he considered them as separate entities, otherwise the count would be eleven. But for all practical purposes they cannot be considered in isolation."[20]

Major Campuzano is a bit of a show-off and a rogue. He marries Doña Estefanía de Caicedo, a woman of loose morals who promises him fidelity and assures him that she has reformed, and further induces him to matrimony by exhibiting her expensive jewels and finery. But after the marriage Doña Estefanía disappears, taking with her the pitifully small fortune of poor Campuzano and leaving him ill with a nasty venereal disease. He lands in the hospital. While undergoing treatment there, in a moment of delirium or in a feverish dream, he thinks he hears two dogs talk. A double irony: the deceiver turns out to be deceived; and the human being who tells his friend Peralta this sad tale then proceeds to give him a manuscript in which he wrote down the conversation of the two dogs—who turn out to be much wiser than the human being who listened to them and even presumably than the human being who reads about this conversation or the other human beings who now read it in the text published by Cervantes. The fact that *Don Quixote* contains two dream sequences (the episode of the wineskins, I, 35, and the vision at the cave of Montesinos, II, 22-24) only reinforces the importance of this strange tale. As J. B. Avalle-Arce explains, "the actual world in which the *Alférez* (Major) Campuzano lives is full of trickery, deceit, hypocrisy and self-interest. As a man who possesses such qualities and tries to make his living through their practice, Campuzano cannot bring himself to recognize this fully, much as Don Quixote cannot reconcile himself, fully, to the disappearance of the chivalresque virtues. But they both dream, and their dreams betray them. The world of Campuzano's dream (that is to say, the actual *Dogs' Colloquy*) is also filled with trickery, deceit, hypocrisy, and self-interest. Through the comments of Berganza we gain an inside view into Campuzano's world, one that he was not willing to admit, as is the case of Don Quixote in the Cave of Montesinos."[21]

Cervantes thus makes an ironical and allegorical tale reveal the subconscious mind of his hero—in this case the sad major. The fact that this story was written several hundred years before Freud should not surprise us. Other great writers (Dostoevski comes to mind immediately) would yield similar examples. Intuition has long preceded psychoanalysis.

The paradox here is that the tale about the two dogs and their conversation is a most implausible dream, a delirium of a sick man who in turn is a fictional character—and yet what the dogs talk about contains more truth than the average conversations in the day of an average man of Cervantes' time or, for that matter, our own time.

What the dog Berganza tells his friend, the dog Cipión, is a sad tale about corruption, folly, virtue unrewarded. (Cipión is a good listener and only from time to time interrupts the unfolding story of Berganza's life with bitter philosophical opinions.) The butchers of Seville, the city where Berganza begins his canine odyssey, steal the best cuts of meat in order to give them to their mistresses: they rob their customers blind. Berganza, who was working as their watchdog, quits in disgust. He then finds employment among some shepherds—who, unlike the shepherds in pastoral novels, are dirty and greedy. They also steal: they claim the wolves kill their sheep in order to find an alibi for their crimes. Berganza leaves them for a merchant. As a pet to his sons, he partakes of the delights of student life. Yet, having quarreled with a female servant, he leaves the household. The tale unfolds further, a variegated tapestry of picaresque life. A canine picaroon, he serves many masters in succession. A corrupt police inspector in cahoots with prostitutes and thieves and good friend of Monipodio, the lord of gangsters, is his next master (here Cervantes anticipates Balzac in having a character from a novel reappear, however briefly, in a subsequent novel). Then a soldier teaches the dog a few tricks that make him almost a circus star, after which he comes under the influence of Cañizares, a gifted and famous warlock. Then come gypsies, actors, etc. Everywhere there is hunger, misery, pettiness. Is this a picaresque novel? The contents are for the most part very similar to the picaresque tales of the period: social satire is sharp and biting. Men are so wicked and perverse that the dog draws back from them repeatedly and tries to escape, only to fall again into their clutches. Disenchantment and bitterness are universal facts of life.

Yet Cervantes' tale transcends the picaresque framework. It is more philosophical, less one-sided, more humorous and satirical. Moreover, the canine hero never loses track of his own moral values. Once more, Cervantes proves in this tale—as in many others of his short stories—that he can put to good use the fashionable literary tastes of his period without being a slave to their formulas: on the contrary, he can—whenever he so chooses—go miles, and even centuries, beyond these formulas. He is truly a modern writer making occasional use of old frameworks.

CHAPTER 6

Cervantes as a Novelist: La Galatea

I A Lifelong Ambition

C ERVANTES started his literary career in earnest as a novelist by publishing *La Galatea* in 1585. He had just settled down in Madrid, five years after returning to Spain from his captivity in Algiers. From that moment until the end of his life, he would never stop writing fiction or thinking about the problems of fiction. Fiction, not poetry or the stage, was his most enduring love. It is unnecessary to insist at this point that whatever Cervantes' worth as a poet or a dramatist, his principal contribution has been undeniably in his mastery of the novel. He completely dominates the field of the modern novel, is the creator who gives birth to several novelistic forms, and as author of *Don Quixote*, is responsible for the most celebrated, penetrating, and original novel of his period.

But the road leading to this literary summit was neither easy nor quick. *La Galatea* was his first novelistic effort, by no means an entirely successful one. Scholars have debated the date of its composition without reaching any agreement. Some scholars, for instance, claim he wrote this novel during his early youth. F. Rodríguez Marín assumes he had written it before 1575, the date of Cervantes' capture, whereas L. Astrana Marín believes that at least part of the work was written in Algiers. Yet the majority of specialists seem to agree that Cervantes wrote the novel after his return from captivity. In any case, this book coincides with the beginning of his literary career: when he published it, he was known only as a poet — and also as the author of a few plays that have been lost and are known to us only insofar as Cervantes himself mentions them. He was at this time thirty-eight years old; for many years *La Galatea* was to remain his only novel.

The novel was published in the city of Alcalá de Henares, not far from Madrid, a city where Cervantes had spent some time in his youth and probably still had a few friends at that moment. It is divided into six books, and the author did not title it "novel," but "eclogue," since it belongs to the pastoral genre, a very popular genre among the reading public of that period.

This genre had been introduced in Spain with the appearance of *Diana* by Jorge de Montemayor in 1558 or 1559: it was to prove of enduring popularity. In a certain sense, it came to replace the declining vogue of the novels of chivalry. In spite of its popularity, the pastoral novel probably never reached as broad a public as the earlier novels of chivalry. Without the marvelous adventures of the early tales, much tamer in their action and more polished in their style, the pastoral novels must have reached only the more cultivated milieux. Nevertheless, in their brief summit of popularity they elicited the serious attention of moralists, and undeniable proof of their influence.

The bucolic or pastoral genre constitutes a genuine literary manifestation of the Renaissance, which until then had been chiefly expressed in the field of lyrical poetry. It represented perhaps the most notable and complete resurrection of the spirit of classical antiquity: the pastoral was a creation of the Greek and Roman civilization and had found in Theocritus and Vergil its finest examples. The Middle Ages continued the bucolic tradition along various lines and with varying enthusiasm. The pastorals of Provence and many forms of Galician-Provençal poetry had preserved it in a certain fashion until Petrarch, with his *Carmen Bucolicum*, modified and modernized this enduring current, finding his inspiration mainly in Vergil, and preparing thus its full development in the sixteenth century in all European literatures. In Spain the pastoral form has its great examples in the *serranillas*, songs dealing with shepherdesses, written by the Archpriest of Hita and the Marquis of Santillana, the latter ones much more polished and elegant.

This pastoral mood favored by Petrarch was oriented towards the novel by his contemporary Boccaccio in two of his works, the *Ninfale d'Ameto* and the *Ninfale fiesolano* (*The Nymph Grove of Ameto*, *The Nymph Grove of Fiesole*). The first one, written in prose interspersed with some poems, is clearly a novel, a new genre of novel: the pastoral novel. During the first years of the sixteenth century, another Italian, the Neapolitan Giacopo Sannazaro, published the most famous pastoral novel of the Renaissance, *Arcadia*, which broadened and established the genre in all its essential characteristics, and which was a close model for the Spanish *Diana* by Jorge de Montemayor.

The bucolic novel, then, as it had been established by Sannazaro, is a genre parallel in prose to the Italianate pastoral poetry. We may say that it is an essentially poetic novel, refined and literary; the shepherds, its protagonists, are not realistically portrayed, but are cultivated, delicate beings, idealized just as in Vergil and in Garcilaso, and totally committed to lament their pangs of love, a love generally frustrated and never reciprocated; Nature, which is also as a rule idealized, is an important component of the whole, much more than a mere background to the painting.

The appearance of mythological characters is frequent. All feelings are tinted with soft and melancholy sadness. We should add that, in general, these novels deal with chaste love affairs. The authors strove to create a climate of virtuous love in which the Platonic ideals of the period could flourish. Everyday life was often in sharp contrast to these Platonic ideals, and the readers knew it; it did not seem to matter. So much the better: a contrast was needed. The times were energetic, superactive, and, perhaps because of it, the readers felt a nostalgia for an idyllic peace. The eulogies, which were in part a literary cliché from classical antiquity, to the quiet life, were an essential part of the pastoral. It is significant that Don Quixote, disenchanted with his adventures and close to death, should seize the idea of becoming a shepherd and compose poems to Dulcinea. In any case, one thing can be said about the pastoral novel: it channels the attention of its readers towards the subtle charms of the inner life. In spite of its conventions, its artificial rhetoric, its excessive idealizations, the pastoral novel deals for the first time, and not always clumsily, with an analysis of the inner life of its characters.

Although Cervantes' novel contains elements which distinguish it from other pastoral novels, perhaps its main trait is that it unites many of the characteristic features of novels of this kind. The main action is very simple. Elicio, a shepherd who dwells on the banks of the river Tagus, is in love with the shepherdess Galatea, who is as famous for her beauty as for her wisdom. Aurelio, father of the beauty, wishes to marry her to a rich shepherd, Erastro, and refuses to heed Elicio's suit. When Elicio learns that his rival is to arrive within three days, he gathers together all his friends in order to beg Aurelio that he not consent to the departure of Galatea, who would thus "divest from those meadows her incomparable beauty." We never learn the results of their joint request because the published portion of the novel ends at this point. However, together with this brief situation, Cervantes introduces a multitude of secondary plots in which the protagonists are, once more, shepherds and shepherdesses who are friends of Galatea's lover. These subplots are so varied and numerous that on occasion they seem to constitute an impenetrable morass.

In weaving these subplots, the novelist resorts to every kind of literary trick — casual discoveries, surprise meetings, mistakes based on the appearance of characters — and all of this takes place in an atmosphere of idealized, Platonic, yet passionate love, a love which is far more often frustrated than reciprocated.

II   *The Rules of the Game*

As usual in novels of this genre, we are dealing here with a *roman à clef*, as Cervantes himself advises us in the preface. After apologizing for "having introduced philosophical ideas among the thoughts of shepherds, who usually deal with problems connected with the earth, and do so in a simple language," he hints that "many of these shepherds in disguise were shepherds only in this disguise."[1] Many scholars have exerted their wits and erudition in a so far vain effort to identify these false shepherds. This problem has actually no bearing on the aesthetic, literary qualities of Cervantes' novel.

It is also in the tradition of other pastoral novels that Cervantes inserts in his *Galatea* many minor poems. He was to follow this tradition in all the novels he wrote, but this he did excessively in the *Galatea;* we have almost eighty poems inserted in the text, and among these a long composition, "Song to Calliope."

The title given by the author, *First Part of the Galatea,* indicates clearly that Cervantes was thinking about a second part to this novel. He mentions this second part, as a project and a promise to his readers, time and time again: in Chapter VI of the first part of *Don Quixote,* the priest states, "It is necessary to wait for the second part of *La Galatea,* which its author has promised us." As late as four days before his death, in his preface to *Persiles,* Cervantes still dreams about completing his first novel: "if by chance or by good luck, which would not be good luck but rather a miracle, I were given an extension on life by divine grace, you will be able to see my new works, and also the second part of *Galatea*."[2] It is obvious here the esteem that Cervantes felt then for his first novel. The pastoral theme comes to the surface in several other sections of his work, and in particular we find in his *Don Quixote* several modalities of this genre. The literary pastoral is to be found in the episode of Marcela and Grisóstomo, the rustic pastoral appears in Camacho's Wedding, and the courtly pastoral in the episode where shepherdesses hunt birds with nets. This sustained interest in the pastoral theme and the fact that the author insists on promising a second part to *Galatea* leads us to think that this novel was not a mere whim of his early years. And yet we should also be aware of the irony with which Cervantes approaches bucolic narration in his *The Dogs' Colloquy*, which has been often taken as proof of his opinion with respect to this sort of idealized fantasy: "Among other things (Berganza said) I thought that what I have heard about the life of shepherds could not possibly have been true . . . they claimed that they passed their lives away by singing and playing bagpipes, fiddles and cymbals, and other strange instruments . . ."[3] It was obvious that the only shepherds that Berganza the dog ever saw were not singing "with sweet melodious voices, but rather with voices so rough that, one by one or in chorus, they did not seem to be singing, but rather screaming or grunting. The greater part of the day was spent defleaing themselves or patching up their rough sandals. Nor did they call each other Amaryllis, Philidas, Galatea, and Diana, nor were there any Lisardos, Lausos, Jacintos, or Riselos; their names were all such as Anthony, Paul, Domingo, or Laurent, whereby I came to understand what I think everybody believes, that is to say, that all these books are made up of fantasies and slick texts written to amuse the idle and hold not a grain of truth. . ."[4]

We are therefore facing a contradiction between Cervantes' theoretical mind and his common sense as expressed in the quotation above. No wonder this contradiction has given rise to one of the most debated problems with respect to Cervantes' true beliefs not only with respect to *Galatea*, but also concerning his "realism." The established, traditional opinion on this matter, one held by Marcelino Menéndez y Pelayo among others, would be as follows: Cervantes, when he wrote *Galatea*, allowed himself to be carried away by the literary fashion of the times, a period in which the pastoral genre was highly appreciated. This attitude of imitation and reverence for the established fashion can be explained in part by the author's youth. Idealism was in the air. Plato was the guiding light of both philosophers and writers. The pastoral genre offered a glimpse of Paradise, a surcease from the tensions of history. One more factor that may have pushed Cervantes to search along the direction of the pastoral genre was that he may have written a number of short poems that he had been unable to publish. Why not write a novel in which they would find a secure place? The prose fiction could thus become a vehicle for his poetry.

Yet the problem is too complex for such a simple solution. Some critics, like Américo Castro, try to find it in a different approach. They think that Cervantes felt equally the attraction of the ideal world and that of the immediate, tangible, everyday world. In this respect he would have been typical of the Renaissance man with his mixed allegiance to different ideals, twin goals. Cervantes had been educated in Platonic thought, and for him there existed an ideal reality with the same clarity as the everyday humble reality around him. It enclosed a world of perfect values which could not be denied or contradicted by what was imperfect, fleeting, actual. Its reality depended in part on its being present in the mind of those happy few who were aware of it. This ideal world could only be contained and expressed fully in the world of art. To enter into it presupposed a prior renunciation of the immediate goals of power, fortune, influence, money, etc., which the everpresent "lowly reality" offered. Hence a disenchanted, ironical viewpoint of Cervantes with respect to pastoral fiction. This enormous and anguishing antagonism between what was real and what was ideal created tension and a by-product of bitterness: Cervantes would have liked, of course, "to eat his cake and have it too," to partake of high Platonic goals and of mundane success.

The contradiction was ultimately solved, as we may now begin to suspect, in the complicated, contradictory, yet artistically satisfactory framework of *Don Quixote*. Yet at first, in *Galatea*, he offers us a pure, clean ingredient, one which by itself is almost inert, ineffectual, passive: Platonic beauty, Neoplatonic love, Nature as a background to human love. It is as if we were preparing an experiment in chemistry, but our homework were incomplete: only one ingredient was at hand, the chemical reaction could not take place. A chemical body can be pure yet ineffectual, inert. In *Don Quixote* this very same ingredient, Platonic ideals, will be able to combine with its opposite, it will be corroded by the acid of everyday life, and then the chemical reaction will take place.

With greater or lesser perspicuity, there is hardly a critic of Cervantes who has not pointed out in some way this duality which rends his character and which is revealed in works apparently so contradictory as *Don Quixote* and *Galatea.* It is true that for many critics the pastoral dream of Cervantes seems to have been a youthful disease, yet a deeply-rooted affliction, one from which he never managed to be completely cured. Yet there are many others who deem the poetic or fantastic works of Cervantes to be of very high quality. For them it cannot be said that Cervantes has wandered through the Arcadian sentimental wastelands and arrived finally at his true goal, his gift for realism, since he dreamed of *Galatea* all his life, and, moreover, he was able to write after *Don Quixote* an idealized novel, *Persiles,* which was in many ways a journey back to his point of departure. There is therefore no linear progression going upwards towards a modern realism. Cervantes traces a zigzag line, one that takes one big step forward and one or two steps backward.

We may ask ourselves why an author who knew so well how to portray his times and the souls of his contemporaries could also be so attracted to the pastoral game. Where does the contradiction begin? We must admit that Cervantes, who possessed such a remarkable intuition with respect to reality, also kept deeply hidden within him a constant attraction to the realm of pure fantasy. His spirit, which was so adept at portraying external reality in succinct prose, could still at times let itself be swept away towards the clouds of fantasy and must have felt the keen necessity of creating a false reality in which to take refuge, one that was more serene, more pleasant, than the bitter reality of everyday life that he knew so well. As a young man, this dream world was the world of the pastoral with its singing shepherds. As an old man, he loved to create tales about travels in mysterious lands and impossible adventures. In both cases, the need to escape was paramount in his mind.

This thread of fantasy can be found in *Galatea,* in the plays, in the *Exemplary Novels,* and, of course, also in *Don Quixote.* It permeates his last work, *Persiles.* Art was for Cervantes a closed world, a secret room where everything could take place. It had its own laws, not quite the same as the laws that ruled mere mortals in their normal lives. It could be made the object of mockery or ridicule, but it would endure: it was eternal, indestructible. Poets were the only mortal beings who could dwell in that lofty room for a limited time. Readers might be made aware of some of the rules and beauties of art, yet most readers could not by themselves endure the tense atmosphere of the closed room with its blinding Platonic light.

An undeniable fact remains: *Galatea* is not a novel that will satisfy or please most modern readers. Even among Spanish readers, presumably more in tune with Cervantes' cultural background and certainly more capable than most foreign readers of appreciating the beauty of its style, it is not easy to find enthusiasts for *Galatea*. Most cultivated Spaniards are aware of its existence and have perhaps read a few paragraphs just as homework for some literature course.

As the critic Agustín González de Amezúa states: "The obvious defects of *Galatea*, its descriptions of pastoral love affairs which are on the whole cold, devoid of passion; the way in which its episodes intertwine, making it difficult to follow its plot; its tendency towards melodrama; the lack of true emotion; an excess of aesthetic speeches on Love that smack of books, not of experience; all these faintings, tears, and sighs; the absence of a true feeling for Nature, seen through artificial and forced descriptions; all these characteristics did not bode well for the success of this novel. All this in spite of the virtues and merits of this work: the dignity and nobility of its characters, some good poems, among the best Cervantes ever wrote, and an elegant style, a style that is worthy of the prince of Castilian prose writers. The fact that during the sixteenth century this novel did not manage to get beyond its second printing is the clearest proof of its literary failure."[5]

If we must look for a redeeming grace in this novel, therefore, we can find it only in its style, and the best way to enjoy it is by listening to its music. The modern reader should prepare himself by reading first a few fragments from Plato's *Dialogues*, a few sonnets by Petrarch, and then step into a beautiful garden and have an actor or an actress with a good voice read aloud the Spanish text. Far away in a grove, a group of madrigal singers should sing. It does not matter whether the listener understands Spanish or not: in this case, the medium — Cervantes' style, the melody of its words, the subtle combination of long and short sentences, the elegance that flows from the subconscious mastery of sounds and rhythms — is the message.

As for the plots themselves, they are both complementary and contradictory. Love scenes abound, yet also violence, suffering, death. As a contemporary critic, Francisco López Estrada, points out, "Cervantes attempts to coordinate the peaceful mood of his shepherds with the violent gusts of tragic clashes. It is not merely the tragedy that can be found in the constant menace of death through unrequited love, ever present among the shepherds . . . Cervantes seems to delight in bloody scenes. He does not avoid the moments of cruelty nor the description of horrible spectacles. Such is, for instance, the scene of the 'bloody kiss' in the tale of Leonida and Lisandro or the parade to a place of execution in the tale of Timbrio and Silerio."[6] (Leonida is loved by Lisandro, a young shepherd; their families are feuding; Leonida's brother sets a trap for the young lovers, has her stabbed; in the dark, the meeting of the two lovers finally takes place: "I groped my way towards the spot where Leonida was lying in a pool of her own blood, and having recognized her immediately I threw myself over her wounded body expressing my grief the best I could. I said to her, 'What misfortune is this, my beloved, my soul? Whose was the cruel hand that had so little respect for so much beauty?' With these words Leonida recognized me and raising with great effort her tired arms she threw them around my neck and embracing me with all the strength she could muster, pressing her lips against mine, in a weak almost inaudible voice she said only this to me: 'My brother has killed me. Carino has betrayed me. Livio is dead. I hope you go on living, my Lisandro, for many happy years. I hope I can enjoy in the afterlife the peace that has been denied me here.' And pressing again her lips to mine, having closed her lips in order to give me her first and her last kiss, when she opened them again her soul flew out and she died in my arms."[7] Melodrama is an everpresent ingredient in these dramatic scenes, and the reaction of the shepherds-actors is always close to overacting: "When I realized what had happened, I almost fainted on top of that cold body. I remained senseless as if I, instead of being alive, were the one who had just died. Anyone who saw us then would have remembered the sad story of Pyramus and Thysbe."[8]

Most of these dramatic incidents are Cervantes' own contribution to the pastoral genre and add a note of pathos to the saccharine dialogues of shepherds in love. Perhaps the author was aware that a note of death, tragedy, blood, would be a welcome antidote to the music of Platonic love. In any case, Cervantes is much more original, in the general composition of his novel, and in many of its incidents, than he has been given credit for in the past. Most critics thought until recently that he had been inspired mainly by Sannazaro's *Arcadia*. The inspiration cannot be discarded, but it affects mainly the mood, the climate, not the plot and the incidents.

The influence of Sannazaro over Cervantes must then be considered rather minor. Other authors, however, may have been more influential, especially the Neoplatonic writings of León Hebreo, the author of *Diálogos de Amor* (*Dialogues about Love*). Cervantes glosses and paraphrases Hebreo's definitions about love, its origins, its consequences. Cervantes borrows ideas and occasionally whole sentences not only from Hebreo, but also from several Italian writers, especially Pietro Bembo, the delicate and elegant follower of Petrarch.

With respect to the importance of the psychological elements in the pastoral novel, and especially in *Galatea,* the contemporary critic Américo Castro has offered several interesting opinions. The pastoral, he points out, has often been interpreted as merely a literary fashion, one that seems to have vanished without trace. This, Castro claims, is an oversimplification or perhaps a mistake. He insists on the importance that the pastoral novel would come to have for the technique, to be found in so many modern novels, of psychological introspection. Shepherds and shepherdesses are always questioning themselves, analyzing their feelings, looking for nuances in their passions or their sentiments. "If one can speak of a source for *Don Quixote,* it must be sought not in the novels of chivalry, nor in Ariosto, nor in the Italian *novellas,* because these possible sources, in spite of their great importance, lacked what we may call 'quixotic possibility'. . . . It is in the pastoral tales where for the first time literary characters appear as strictly human individuals, as the expression of inner feelings. We have spoken too much about the abstract and conventional nature of the pastoral genre, about its carelessness about time and space, and this prevented us from paying attention to the inner dimension of its characters: the inner space is the only space where they exist. It does not matter that the love of these shepherds in these 'pastoral erotic novels' be a mere optical illusion, since thanks to such an illusion the sensitive awareness of each character emerges as autonomous and dominant."[9]

Another critic, the Italian Paolo Savj-Lopez, has also pointed out the importance of the pastoral for the development of our modern novels: "A devotee of literary paradox could claim that the modern novel derives from the *Arcadia*. If the *Arcadia* inspired *Diana* by Montemayor, and from this last novel is derived *L'Astrée*, and from *L'Astrée* through Prévost, Marivaux, Le Sage, one comes to the English novel of Richardson and of Fielding, we have then reached exactly the modern novel. And in the background, far away, emerges the giant shadow of Giovanni Boccaccio, who links with this chain of narrative works not through the powerful human reality of his *Decameron*, but through the pastoral allegorical visions of his *Ninfale d'Ameto*, the closest and direct begetter of Sannazaro's *Arcadia*."[10]

Cervantes' version of the pastoral does not exclude adventure, intrigue, lofty conversations in which shepherds and shepherdesses discuss the origins of Platonic love. Some fragments of it can still be read with pleasure. Yet on the whole we are tempted to state that the true merit of this novel is that it trained Cervantes as a novelist. It was an exercise in a long apprenticeship: it was Cervantes' first novel. Moreover, it trained his mind and sensitivity towards the description of the inner life of his characters: introspection, inwardness are the hallmarks of this novel, and through these traits the novel can still be said to be worthy of our attention. The pastoral genre was for Cervantes a lasting obsession: time and time again it would reappear in his writings, either directly or through some allusion. Yet when it does reappear in *Don Quixote*, it does so in a framework that has been thoroughly changed, modernized, made more sophisticated. The twenty years that separate *Galatea* from the first part of *Don Quixote* seem more like two hundred years to a modern reader: such is the leap in complexity and depth that separates these two novels.

CHAPTER 7

Cervantes's Masterpiece:
Don Quixote

I A Mature Work

CERVANTES was fifty-seven years old when the first part
of *The Ingenious Gentleman Don Quixote de la Mancha* was
printed in Madrid, in 1605, in the printing presses of Juan de la
Cuesta, and distributed by the publisher and bookseller Francisco de
Robles. This novel interrupted a long silence. For twenty years Cervantes had published nothing. This does not mean that he had given
up literature. He had written some of his *Exemplary Novels*—and
put them away in a drawer. He had written a few plays—and had
been unable to have them accepted by any stage company; his plays
remained unperformed. Yet Cervantes was not easily discouraged.

Cervantes' novel was dedicated to Don Alonso Diego López de
Zúñiga y Sotomayor, Duke of Béjar. It was the well-established
custom of the time, and an economic necessity for a writer who tried
to live by his pen, to secure a patron for an important book. There
were no royalties, and all that a writer could expect was the modest
sale price of his manuscript and whatever gift of money the patron
might feel inclined to offer. Cervantes' patron seems to have been
less than generous. At any rate, Cervantes never dedicated another
book to him. We do not know how much Francisco de Robles paid
for the manuscript of *Don Quixote*. We suspect the sum was rather
modest. It was probably used to defray the costs of Cervantes' moving to Valladolid.

As Cervantes penned the Prologue to his novel, he must have
reflected how old and tired he was, how improbable it appeared that
the new book would accomplish what his other works had been incapable of bringing him: fame—and a little money. Yet he always

knew how to mask his anguish behind a cordial smile and a hint of mockery at the pedants. In his Prologue he pretends he does not know what to say or how he could dare to publish a book which is so unadorned with the learned trappings which other authors favor and which lend authority to their publications: "On one occasion when I was thus in suspense, paper before me, pen over my ear, elbow on the table, and chin in hand, a very clever friend of mine came in. Seeing me lost in thought, he inquired as to the reason . . ." Cervantes explains why he is so worried: "How, I said to him, can you expect me not to be concerned over what that venerable legislator, the Public, will say when it sees me, at my age, after all these years of silent slumber, coming out with all my years on my back, with a tale that is dried as a rush, a stranger to invention, paltry in style, impoverished in content, and wholly lacking in learning and wisdom, without quotations in the margins or notes at the end of the book; when other books of this sort, even though they be fabulous and profane, are so packed with maxims from Aristotle and Plato and the whole crowd of philosophers as to fill the reader with admiration and lead him to regard the author as a well-read, learned, and eloquent individual?"[1]

Cervantes could not pass up any occasion to attack pedantry and inflated egos. Not even while he was trying to make friends for his new book. He must have realized that writing the preface to *Don Quixote* marked an important moment in his life. He was coming out of his long silence, his protracted hibernation: a mature writer, in full possession of his art, yet unknown as a writer, for all practical purposes ignored or neglected until that moment by readers and critics alike. There was no bitterness or self-reproach in his tone. He had lost many literary battles—his *Galatea* had largely failed to find an audience, his poems, he knew, were not first-rate, his early plays lay in oblivion, his new plays could not find an audience—but he had not lost the war.

II *Parody or Self-Portrait?*

Don Quixote is a long, rich, complex novel. The fifty-two chapters of the first part constitute a book of considerable bulk. Cervantes' technique as a novelist is both bold and refined, often strikingly original.

This is why we cannot grasp immediately the unique qualities of the novel: no brief definition will do. We must approach the novel as a whole—and specifically what we think may have been Cervantes' conception of *Don Quixote*, his intention—with care, perhaps follow an oblique or roundabout path. Let us examine first two basic—we are almost tempted to write simplistic—approaches to our novel. The first approach sees in *Don Quixote* mainly a parody of the romances of chivalry. The second tries to define the novel in terms of a disguised autobiography of Cervantes. There is some truth in both. After we become acquainted with these approaches, we shall add several other interpretations, some of them divergent, others complementary. The analytic canvas will become thus more and more crowded, more detailed, more complete. We shall in this manner, hopefully, come closer to the truth.

Cervantes' hypothetical friend seems quite sure of *Don Quixote's* intent: "Let it be your aim that, by reading your story, the melancholy may be moved to laughter and the cheerful man made merrier still; let the simple not be bored, but may the clever admire your originality; let the grave ones not despise you, but let the prudent praise you. And keep in mind, above all, your purpose, which is that of undermining the ill-founded edifice that is constituted by those books of chivalry, so abhorred by many but admired by many more; if you succeed in attaining it, you will have accomplished no little."[2] This text is part of the Preface to Part I. Nowadays most novels dispense with a preface. At that time a preface was almost indispensable: it introduced the novel to the reader, it explained the author's purpose, it gave a general idea of what the novel was about. It did not describe the plot, except in the vaguest terms, yet it set the tone, the mood—much like an opera's overture. There were no critical notes in newspapers or magazines, no television interviews, no blurbs in books' jackets: the preface had to accomplish a public relations job, a general description and self-appraisal that today's authors accomplish in many other fashions. This is why Cervantes' Preface is interesting and important—and also why we would be wrong to accept it at face value. What reader or critic accepts without question what the jacket says about the contents and the value of a novel?

Cervantes' message in the lines quoted above seems to be, "This is an amusing book. It will make you laugh. It is a parody (a parody of the romances of chivalry, known to everybody, therefore it is a parody easy to understand, one which will not be lost on the average reader), and by definition all parodies are funny. It is an original parody lampooning a subject that needs to be laughed at: the books of chivalry were "abhorred by many," that is to say, they were criticized without mercy by solemn Christian moralists and Aristotelian critics. The first found them a waste of time and often, moreover, complained about these romances being larded with immoral erotic scenes. The second found them full of erroneous observations, lacking in verisimilitude, in a word, childish.

Cervantes was well aware of these criticisms: he knew, moreover, that the average reader of *Don Quixote* would probably have read one or two romances of chivalry at least—or perhaps one or two dozen, like Don Quixote himself. Yet he was also conscious of the fact that the readers were becoming more sophisticated, more adult in their taste: they were beginning to see through the impossible and incredible situations offered by these books, and were also beginning to reject the demands for a "suspension of disbelief" that such novels made continually on their public. A good parody, a successful parody, must start with the premise that the object of parody is well known to the reader or the spectator: this is the assumption made by Cervantes. Moreover, the author of a parody must assume that the identification between reader or spectator and the object of parody is not at the moment too close, too intimate: otherwise, parody misses the point and produces indignation instead of humor. Cervantes was also fairly certain that this was the case: Spanish readers of the upper classes, readers with a certain degree of culture and sophistication, had already become suspicious of romances of chivalry; the lowbrow readers (and Cervantes will introduce one such reader, the Innkeeper, in his novel) were slowly becoming suspicious, and yet they were not always ready to disbelieve in their heroes.

In any case, Cervantes states his intention in such a clear way that he leaves no doubt to his contemporary public as to what his aim is: he wants to expose once and for all the weaknesses of a hitherto admired literary genre. His statement carries the day: he convinced most of his readers—and the impact of his remarks continued to be felt century after century.

The principal idea that the average reader had then—and perhaps still has today—about *Don Quixote* is that it is basically a parody of the romances of chivalry, and although it is undeniable that this interpretation is immediately belied by even the most superficial analysis of Cervantes' novel, it is nonetheless certain that a brief synopsis of *Don Quixote* cannot avoid conveying such an impression. This might be taken to be undeniable proof that such a burlesque intention is to be found at least in the initial conception of the book. It can be affirmed that Cervantes' contemporaries at first saw only the vein of humor, absurdity, and laughter uncovered by the adventures of the hidalgo and his squire. The immense popularity of both master and servant and their no less famous mounts can be explained by the opportunity for merriment that these characters provided. Cervantes himself, in the second part of his book, states this fact through one of his characters, Sansón Carrasco: talking about the success of the novel's first part, he states that "little children leaf through it, young people read it, adults appreciate it, and the aged sing its praises. In short, . . . it is so thumbed and read and so well known to persons of every walk in life that no sooner do folks see some skinny nag that they at one cry, 'There goes Rocinante!' "[3] The knight himself restates and reinforces the definition of the novel as a humorous book: "to sum up the matter, Señor Bachelor, it is my opinion that, in composing histories or books of any sort, a great deal of judgment and ripe understanding is called for. To say and write witty and amusing things is the mark of great genius. The cleverest character in a comedy is the clown, since he who would make himself out to be a simpleton cannot be one."[4] Cervantes, as is often the case, tries to communicate with two different types of readers, and therefore offers two messages. He must restate his main message: his book is a humorous parody. The second message, addressed to the most sophisticated readers and critics, is simply that in his humorous parody there is more than meets the eye: a great deal of art and wisdom entered into its composition. Critics may complain, they may find the book shallow or faulty; they would make a mistake. It would be a not unusual mistake: "printed works being read at leisure, their faults are the more readily apparent, and the greater the reputation of the author the more closely are they scrutinized. Men famous for their genius, great poets, illustrious historians, are almost always envied by those who take a special delight in criticizing the writings of others without having produced anything of their own."[5]

No matter how much critics might complain, Cervantes was sure of reaching a faithful group of readers, made up of all the ex-devotees of chivalry romances, all the readers who, avid of emotion and adventure, but not having given up their critical senses, had enjoyed these romances but were also ready to laugh at them and to feel superior to their original enthusiasm. Readers, Cervantes knew, are fickle: they are easily swayed by fashions. The literary fashion of chivalry had reached its peak: it was time for parody. He so states at the end of the whole novel, in the final chapter of the second part: "For the two sallies that [Don Quixote] did make to the delight and approval of all who heard of them, in foreign countries as well as our own, are sufficient to cast ridicule upon all the ridings forth of knights-errant in times past . . . . I have had no other purpose than to arouse the abhorrence of mankind toward those false and nonsensical stories to be met with in the books of chivalry, which, thanks to this tale of the genuine Don Quixote, are already tottering and without a doubt are doomed to fall."[6]

Nothing could be clearer, more explicit, apparently final: Cervantes tells us exactly what he intended to do in his novel. And furthermore, Cervantes' contemporaries seem to have understood this purpose quite clearly. A great Spanish playwright of the time, and also a sincere admirer of Cervantes, Tirso de Molina, defined Cervantes as "the implacable expeller of errant knights."

Obviously there is more than a kernel of truth in the hypothesis that *Don Quixote* was intended basically as a parody of the romances of chivalry. It is quite possible that this was the conception at the origin of the novel, no matter how much Cervantes enriched, changed, and made more complex this basic idea. We should never forget Cervantes' admiration for Italian culture, Italian literature. One of the curious facts about Italian literature is that it never developed a true epic tradition like the tradition of most other European literatures: Italy has no medieval poem to be compared to *Nibelungen, La Chanson de Roland,* the *Cantar de Mio Cid.* (Dante's *Divine Comedy* is a philosophical poem, not an epic one.) Italian literature was perhaps still under the spell of Greek and Roman tradition: perhaps no Italian writer wished to compete with Homer and Vergil. Be this as it may, the tradition that was developed was one that poked fun at the heroics of Gothic heroes. The mock heroic poems of late Medieval and early

Renaissance times are a feature of Italian culture that has no parallel in the rest of Europe.

Cervantes must have known these poems. He certainly knew and admired the long, beautiful, and complex poem written by Ludovico Ariosto, the *Orlando Furioso (Orlando's Madness)*. Cervantes mentions this poem several times in his novel. He ends the first part of *Don Quixote* by quoting a line from Ariosto's poem: *Fors'altri canterà con miglior plettro* (Perhaps someone else will sing with a better voice). Ariosto's poem is not a mock heroic poem, yet neither is it a true epic poem: It is rather a "poetic romance," showing impetuous romantic action unfolding against a background of legendary struggle. it is a synthesis of a vague, mysterious knightly world deeply engraved in lights and shadows, rich landscapes, and pleasant incongruities. Only the sophisticated art of Ariosto may force us to believe in the reality, or perhaps semireality, of the events described. Ariosto does not aim at psychological verisimilitude or historical truth. Art is his only guide. The reader's experience is a carefully controlled one. Not only are the actors in it fabulous and remote in both time and space; the author appears in his pages time and time again, like a clever puppeteer who at the end of each dramatic scene insists on sharing the applause granted his puppets, and must appear on stage to show us that he is the one who pulls the strings.

Let us remember that the Marxist critic, George Lukács, has called the modern novel—he is speaking about Balzac and his followers, but his ideas apply equally to Cervantes—a "degraded epic," an epic written for and by the bourgeoisie. Let us also point out that Ariosto's epic is not a true epic, but that it is rather a distorted, tongue-in-cheek epic. This will show us in a glimpse that Ariosto's effort is but one first step towards the modern novel. Cervantes was the only one who seems to have understood the possibilities of having a hero that was less than perfect, but thought himself as the heir of fabulous knights. Ariosto's heroes are much too human. They are more cunning than heroic, more lustful than cunning.

Ariosto's poem is entirely different from *Don Quixote* with respect to the style, the characters, and the plot. Nevertheless Cervantes must have sensed its possibilities as a blueprint for a novel, one in which a pseudohero would appear. Ariosto had offered his fairy-tale characters to an adult sophisticated audience. Why not pit a single man, Don Quixote, completely submerged in a fairy-tale atmosphere of legends and lofty principles, against the abrasive and picturesque presence of Spanish everyday life, with its picaresque characters, and with a few middle-class and even upper-class characters thrown in for good measure? That is to say, one lonely individual who did believe in epic legends and traditions against a mass of doubters and non believers. The tables could always be turned against the lonely pseudoknight if he was, to begin with, middle-aged, obscure, obsessed, unrealistic. Yet Cervantes had to take care not to tip the balance too far against Don Quixote. He is provided with a comforting Platonic love, a squire who grows fond of his master, an uncanny ability to endure blows, and a belief in evil magicians that will excuse his constant failures. The match is even: Don Quixote can face his society. He can fight the impossible fight, endure the unendurable blows of destiny. Somehow, perhaps without being fully aware of it, Cervantes is often on the side of his knight: Don Quixote's rivals and critics will often appear to be petty. They burn his books, don ridiculous disguises, lose battles against Don Quixote: they can be just as foolish—but less noble. Thus, as we read on, what started as a cautionary tale becomes more subtle, more ambiguous.

That the relationship between Cervantes and his hero is a strange and wavering one should not come as a surprise to us if we subscribe to the theory that Cervantes was trying to express through him a whole side of his own personality: in other words, that there are autobiographical elements in Cervantes' novel.

As Gerald Brenan develops this theory, he writes: "*Don Quixote* was conceived in prison at a low-water mark in Cervantes' life and he tells us that in writing it he 'gave play to his melancholy and disgrunted feelings.' Something more then than a skit on the novels of Chivalry must have been intended. I think therefore, that we ought to take note of the fact that the famous knight had many features in common with his creator."[7] Many of these features are evident even to the reader who is not a specialist on Cervantes or a professional critic, but who keeps his eyes open. We learn, for instance, that Don Quixote was of the same age as Cervantes when he set out on his adventures. The portraits of Cervantes show him as a man with a narrow and long face, a spacious forehead, somewhat melancholy eyes. Cervantes was the eternal optimist, always ready to crack a joke even during his numerous personal crises. He—like the Spanish generals and admirals, the Spanish king—set out to reform the world by force of arms, and was finally defeated by his adversaries.

"It is true," Gerald Brenan points out, "that these similarities are accompanied by even greater dissimilarities. But if the writer was in some sense 'putting himself' into his hero, that is precisely what we should expect. When novelists seek to create characters who will represent the deepest things in themselves, they start by delineating something very different. It is by wearing masks that one obtains freedom of self-expression. I suggest, therefore, that one of the sources of Don Quixote's power to move us comes from his being a projection of a discarded part of Cervantes himself: that is to say, of the noble intentions and failure of his life."[8]

Of course we should realize that a man as creative as Cervantes—as optimistic, as full of enthusiasm—could not be entirely bitter when dealing with an important "self," with a significant part of his own personality. Hence the ambivalent attitude towards his hero: Cervantes both loved and hated the character he had created. Objectively, Cervantes' life had been a long failure. Subjectively, he was—at least we may assume so—moderately happy and content. The contradiction had to be resolved. If indeed the creation of Don Quixote is not devoid of autobiographical details, it must have been related to an intense effort of self-appraisal and self-definition on the part of Cervantes. This in itself would give Cervantes' hero a complexity, both dramatic and pathetic, which we seldom find in the narrative prose of Golden Age Spain.

III   *The Creation of* Don Quixote

The first chapters of Cervantes' novel contain a number of startling facts. Perhaps most obvious is the lack of precision about the novel's hero. Romances of chivalry usually give us both the name of the hero and his genealogy. The land where he lives, the name of the castle, the name of the king, are carefully written down for the information of the readers. Picaresque novels are also detailed and precise: we know the hero's name, where and how he was born, the circumstances surrounding his birth. Charles Dickens' *David Copperfield* echoes as late as the nineteenth century this rule of precision. Not so Cervantes in his novel. We are told that his hero was born "in a village of La Mancha the name of which I have no desire to recall" (I, 1), and instead of his name we are given a generic—we might almost say sociological—description: "one of those gentlemen who always have a lance in the rack, an ancient buckler, a skinny nag, and a greyhound for the chase" *(Ibid.)*. His normal life is then briefly described: his food, the people around him. It is all hopelessly "middle class," bound by tradition and habit. The gentleman's name is left in doubt: "They will try to tell you that his surname was Quijada or Quesada—there is some difference of opinion among those who have written on the subject—but according to the most likely conjectures we are to understand that it was really Quejana" *(Ibid.)*. It turns out later that perhaps the correct name was not Quejana but Quijano.

This gentleman, whose face is lean and gaunt and whose only pleasure is reading romances of chivalry, is undergoing what we would call nowadays an "identity crisis." Our hero is radically different from other heroes: He is not young, handsome, and dashing; he does not possess the appealing grace of the very young heroes of picaresque novels. He is close on to fifty years. He has become so immersed in his reading that he spends night and day poring over romances of chivalry until "finally, from so little sleeping and so much reading, his brain dried up and he went completely out of his mind" *(Ibid.)*. When his wits are gone beyond repair, he conceives the idea, "in order to win a greater amount of honor for himself and serve his country at the same time, to become a knight-errant and roam the world on horseback, in a suit of armor; he would go in quest of adventures, by way of putting into practice all that he had read in his books; he would right every manner of wrong . . ." *(Ibid.)*. An adolescent dream comes true in the mind of an old gentleman. Alonso Quijano gives birth to Don Quixote in the first chapters of Cervantes' novel. Thus an element of unreality is introduced from the very beginning in a realistic novel: we are dealing with a fictitious character, one that has been superimposed upon an aging *hidalgo* by the will of the *hidalgo*—and of Cervantes. The birth of Don Quixote has been made possible by a complicated chain of circumstances. Alonso Quijano is bored with his monotonous life—and obsessed with the ideal world he has found in the romances of chivalry. Through Alonso Quijano, Cervantes creates Don Quixote as a character whose life is permeated by literature.

Don Quixote is modeled after the hero of one of the most famous romances of chivalry, *Amadís de Gaula (Amadis of Gaul)*, written by Garci Ordóñez de Montalvo. Don Quixote, in a way, is "a man who becomes a book," or at least whose life is modeled after a book. At the same time, Cervantes' negative reaction to the romances of chivalry is based upon Aristotle's *Poetics*, with its emphasis upon verisimilitude, as well as upon the many Neo-Aristotelian Spanish critics of the Golden Age. We are also aware, as we read on in Cervantes' novel, that several chapters are devoted almost exclusively to literary criticism: several secondary characters—the Curate, the Barber, the Canon, among others, and certainly Don Quixote himself—discuss in detail the merits and demerits of books. Slowly a theory of the novel emerges from the pages of this novel. The main character himself, the bookish knight, seems to be an island surrounded by books. It is therefore unavoidable and necessary to examine, however briefly, the literary sources of *Don Quixote*.

IV   Don Quixote *and its Sources*

It is a well-known fact that no writer creates in a vacuum. Even the most original works of art always have precedents, sources that help the writer or the artist in the act of creation. It is not to diminish the merit of Cervantes as the author of *Don Quixote*, but rather with the purpose of better understanding Cervantes' novel and the purpose of its author that we should scan Cervantes' cultural background in seeking the sources of *Don Quixote*.

These sources can be of at least three categories. The first possible source is a hypothetical—and yet quite possible—"real-life Don Quixote." Did Cervantes know some eccentric *hidalgo* that may have served him as a prototype for Don Quixote? It is quite plausible. The Spanish critic M. Menéndez y Pelayo discusses several instances of hallucinations, either comic or tragic, produced by the reading of romances of chivalry. Francisco de Portugal narrates in his *Arte de Galantería (The Art of Good Breeding)* that a Portuguese knight came home once and found his wife, his sons and daughters, and his servants, all crying bitterly. He asked them what was wrong and they answered: "Amadis is dead." Luis Zapata discusses in his *Miscelánea* the case of a knight who was usually normal and peaceful, but who one day suddenly left his home without apparent motive, took off his clothes and killed an ass by a swift thrust of a knife; he began to pursue some peasants, brandishing a stick, imitating the insanities of Orlando, the main character of Ariosto's *Orlando Furioso*.[9]

There existed, therefore, an environment quite favorable to madness in general. Many people lived in a state of perpetual emotional exaltation provoked, in part, by the romances of chivalry. We should not forget that the era was tense for many reasons, political and religious, and superstitions were rife. (The seventeenth century seems obsessed, among other strange beliefs, by the subjects of witchcraft and demonology.)

Many nineteenth-century critics, following the trend of historical and positivistic schools of thought, searched in vain through Spanish archives and medical histories of the period trying to find a real-life model for Don Quixote. We have come to the conclusion that even if such a model existed it would be a waste of time to try to study it: a poor madman would hardly have much in common with Don Quixote's rich and complex personality.

Another type of sources are the literary sources. These could have inspired Cervantes to create situations and characters. For instance: the Spanish critic R. Menéndez Pidal believes a short anonymous play, *Entremés de los Romances (The Farce of Ballads)* could have influenced Cervantes.[10] A short parallel between the two, the farce and the novel, can be useful. In the novel, the knight is driven mad by reading novels of chivalry and he sets out alone on his first expedition in search of adventures. After having been dubbed a knight by the innkeeper and the two prostitutes, he attempts to free a boy who is being whipped by his master, and after this runs into two merchants from Toledo whom he orders to proclaim Dulcinea's beauty; in the brawl that takes place, he falls from his horse and a servant of the merchants beats Don Quixote with his own lance. The knight is stretched out without being able to move, and begins then to recite the ballad about Valdovinos and the Marquis of Mantua:

> Where art thou, lady mine,
> That thou dost not grieve for my woe?
> Either thou are disloyal,
> Or my grief thou dost not know.

He then goes on reciting the whole ballad until he comes to the verses

O noble marquis of Mantua,
My uncle and liege lord true!

The similarities with the play are many. In the play the hero, Bartolo, goes mad by reading ballads. He then becomes a soldier and believes he is a character, Tarfe, out of a ballad with a Moorish theme; he tries to defend a shepherdess pursued by a lad, but is beaten with his own lance; he lies stretched out on the ground; just like Don Quixote, he blames his horse for his fall; then he thinks he is Valdovinos and begins to recite the ballad about the Marquis of Mantua. Many other details seem to coincide with details in the first chapters of *Don Quixote*.

What does it all prove? Very little, perhaps nothing at all. Many scholars are not convinced that the play is older than the novel. The similar details might be due to a simple coincidence. In any case, the similarity in certain details does not go beyond Chapter 7 of the novel. The main character in the play is grotesque, witless, uninspired; not so Don Quixote, whose mind is clear—with the exception of his obsession for knight-errantry—whose speech is eloquent and often elegant, and whose spirit is noble.

Obviously another factor in the genesis of Cervantes' novel can be found in the romances of chivalry. *Don Quixote's* structure is based upon two premises that can be found in the romances of chivalry: the open road and the almost endless string of adventures. Cervantes makes full use of this structure: he simply translates the basic plan of these romances into the key of irony, parody, comic elements, and attitudes. The character of both the knight and his squire is slowly revealed through a flow of incidents: it is quite possible that Cervantes did not envision in his first mental draft his two heroes in their full development and perfectly meshed into a careful plan. However, the episodic unfolding of the novel allowed him to unravel through successive attempts, and by adding new touches, all of the rich potential complexities of personality which lay dormant in his original conception.

This progressive development of characters within the framework of an adventure story not only did not detract from Cervantes' art, but, according to some critics, especially R. Menéndez Pidal, contributed to the excellence of its results: "Far from these adventures being boring repetitions in which a stereotype would repeat itself, they are a continuing revelation, even for their very creator, and thus incessantly surprise the reader. The main character is not completely defined until the very end of the novel."[11]

But all of these adventures which constitute the principal thread of the story are mixed with another series of secondary events and auxiliary tales related more or less closely to the adventures of Don Quixote. This is true for the first part of the novel—the second part has a clearer structure and is devoid of secondary tales. We can also mention the "special chapters," such as the examination of Don Quixote's library, or the speeches by Don Quixote about the Golden Age, on Arms and Letters, and by the Canon and the Curate about books of chivalry and Spanish playwrights. Obviously here the sources are somewhat specialized: for instance, we can imagine Cervantes making use of some of the writings by the Neo-Aristotelian critics of his time, with respect to the literary criticism that appears in several of the incidents above mentioned.

The long tales which Cervantes includes in the first part of the novel have also, of course, literary sources and influences. M. Menéndez y Pelayo has stated that in these episodic tales of the First Part one can find a complete inventory of every literary genre—in prose—that preceded Cervantes, so that merely by reading and analyzing these tales "all of the imaginative literature before Cervantes can be surmised and restored, for Cervantes assimilated and incorporated it all in his work."[12]

For example: We find a pastoral novel—although a miniature one—in the episode of Marcela and Grisóstomo, the first of a series of novelettes placed at the beginning of Part I (Chapters 12 to 14); and in the tale of Leandra (placed very close to the end, Chapter 51), we find another example of pastoral fiction. The so-called "sentimental romance" finds expression in the tales of Cardenio, Lucinda and Dorotea, in the last of which is to be found the influence of the novel, perhaps the best in Spanish literature, *Diana*, by Jorge de Montemayor; Montemayor, in turn, imitated the Italian writer Bandello when writing his chapters on Félix and Felixmena, the two lovers that influence Cervantes in the pastoral tales above mentioned. The psychological novel is illustrated by Cervantes in his tale

of "The Story of the One Who Was Too Curious for his Own Good."
The "contemporary thriller" is illustrated in Cervantes' "The Cap-
tive's Story." All this without mentioning details that remind us of
Ariosto's poem, *Orlando Furioso,* and of Bandello's short stories.

V   *The Novel's Structure*

We can now see that the plan of *Don Quixote,* at least the plan
followed for the First Part of the novel, is based upon a circular
movement. The knight leaves home, has several adventures, then
comes back home; he leaves again, this time accompanied by
Sancho Panza, his adventures unfold and multiply, and are often interrupted by secondary tales. Finally the knight goes home—we
assume forever—at the end of the First Part.

The literary merit of all the secondary episodes has been the subject of several interpretations. In general, although many critics find
them interesting and beautiful as isolated literary compositions, they
are considered out of place. This is why, according to most modern
critics—and also most modern readers—the second part of the novel
is better organized and is superior from a literary viewpoint to the
first part. The episodes of the First Part interrupt the flow of adventures and even the interesting dialogue between Don Quixote and
his squire; they distract the reader's attention.

The question is, why did Cervantes compose his novel in this
manner? The critics who admit Cervantes' vacillation in the creation
and treatment of his hero during this First Part assume that these
novelettes are a subterfuge on the part of an author that occasionally
seems to have lost track of the pulse of his heroes. Thus, a perceptive
critic such as Salvador de Madariaga comments: "This sudden ex-
uberance of tales and episodes at the end of the First Part does not
seem to be the product of a mere abundance of creative energy.
Rather it suggests a certain vacillation on the part of the author with
respect to his main plot. Cervantes seems here to lose for a moment
the thread of his real tale; he seems to fail to see clearly the development of his two main characters. The rapid succession of episodes
which appear in these chapters seems rather like the 'padding' of a
tired author, a pause along the road of creation, a pastime for a tired
imagination that squanders in minor tasks a strength that is already
too weak for its principal task."[13]

These are harsh words. We do not know how Cervantes felt as he proceeded with the writing of his novel. He has left us no diary. Yet another possibility should be taken into account: Cervantes had not lost track of his heroes, he did not lack in interest for them or in creative strength to go on with the main line of adventures, but rather he did not trust the patience of his readers. It is a known fact that the span of attention of many readers, modern or in the seventeenth century, is often not enough to encompass a long novel. Cervantes thought, perhaps, that his readers could become tired of Don Quixote and Sancho; the time had come to introduce new elements, new tales that by their variety and their intrinsic merits would sustain the flagging attention of his readers. He was a born storyteller, he may have written one or several of his short stories even before he started writing his novel: his materials were there, ready, in a drawer; perhaps "padding" is too strong a word in this case; he might have called it "a judicious introduction of variety."

Cervantes himself felt the need to defend the checkered structure of his First Part: He talks about "a kind of grudge . . . against himself for having undertaken a story so dry and limited in scope as is this one of Don Quixote. For it seemed to him [Cervantes] that he was always having to speak of the knight and of Sancho, without being able to indulge in digressions of a more serious and entertaining nature; he remarked that to go on like this, pen in hand, with his mind fixed upon a single subject, and having to speak through the mouths of a few persons only, was for him an intolerable and unprofitable drudgery" (II, 44).

Cervantes is therefore aware of the problem. In the Second Part he has recovered complete control over the main plot, and the creative impulse will proceed in a straight line, with great economy and precision, towards its poignant final climax. Cervantes knows that his main characters do not bore his readers: no secondary tales are needed. But at the same time, he seems to complain about his new Spartan structure: he feels himself capable of creating a sea of tales, a crowd of new characters, and is compelled to limit his imagination. Yet his knight will afford a few occasions in which Cervantes can create short sketches of secondary characters, always properly linked to the adventures of knight and squire. For instance: a letter from Sancho's wife to the squire is the occasion Cervantes needs to create a miniature about country life. Cervantes loves to create new characters: He loves mankind—not as an abstraction, a philosophical or political idea, but as an infinite source of concrete types, of individual and unique characters.

The problem of structuring a long novel around a hero's multiple adventures in a way that does not allow its readers to become bored with the hero is in part a technical one. Cervantes does his best to solve it in the First Part by introducing secondary adventures, in the Second Part by working the lives of secondary characters more closely with the life and adventures of his hero. Basically his solution is artistic and psychological: little by little he discovers that the best way to hold the readers' attention is to make his hero—and his hero's friend, Sancho Panza—as real and as interesting as possible. This is the sudden revelation produced by the appearance of Cervantes' novel: a hero can be created that unfolds and develops along each chapter, becoming someone who is more real to us than most people we happen to know. Spanish literature was no stranger to the kind of work where the hero and the heroine appear as believable characters whom we hate or admire or despise—and who sometimes inspire in us a complex mixture of emotions. La Celestina by Fernando de Rojas (1499) had created an unforgettable go-between, an old woman both wise and despicable: Cervantes was sensitive to the book's charms and defines them succinctly in one of the poems appended to the preface of the First Part: ". . . that divine boo(k), /The Celestina, you choose to loo(k), /Or 'twould be divine if more discree(t)." The Lazarillo de Tormes (1554) had also given its readers a well-rounded type, the resourceful picaroon. These characters were believable partly because of their human weaknesses. Don Quixote would become believable in spite of his idealism, his courage, his chastity. The knight's many virtues are of course real in his mind, they rule each one of his actions—it is only their consequences that are laughable: the discrepancy between moral ends and practical means is a constant source of tension for Don Quixote and constant merriment for the readers. Cervantes solves thus a structural problem that the writers of picaresque novels never knew how to treat adequately. The best-known picaresque novel of Cervantes' era, Guzmán de Alfarache by Mateo Alemán, is heavy on the moralistic side: numerous passages describe the errors in the hero's ways, warn the reader against repeating the picaroon's mistakes. These are pages that a modern reader finds almost unpalatable and that on the whole may have bored not a few Spanish seventeenth-century readers, yet the social and religious morality of the period, not to mention censorship, made them unavoidable. Another picaresque novel of the Spanish Renaissance, *Lazarillo de Tormes,* avoids the excessive buildup of tension and cynicism by the artifice of brevity: its final chapters are very short, the reader has the feeling that its author wants to end as soon as possible a book that has become progressively more dangerous (the fact that the author knew his book contained subversive passages may be surmised by his having remained anonymous.)

Therefore Cervantes' hero would have to be robust enough to carry on his shoulders the weight of a whole long novel—and ethical enough to escape the wrath of the censors and the moralists, yet entertaining enough so that the average reader, always a mixture of cynicism and accepted moral values, could enjoy the knight's adventures. The formula devised by Cervantes is both Christian and Aristotelian: we are asked to laugh not at virtue, but at its excesses. Aristotle had pointed out that courage is the happy middle ground between cowardice and foolhardiness: Don Quixote's courage leans dramatically towards temerity.

One of the secrets of the knight's resilience is, of course, that he is not completely and irreparably mad. He can learn, and occasionally does, from his mistakes. Moreover, the people who surround him can also learn something from his antics, and occasionally Don Quixote becomes a teacher. As Lowry Nelson puts it, "there are, of course, obvious elements of farce: highfalutin names, palpable delusion, mistaken identities, slapstick disasters. But instead of being finally and ignominiously ejected by normal society the protagonist, Don Quijote, creates for himself a whole way of life so consistent and resilient that normal society finds itself variously involved in conforming to its terms, now knowingly indulgent and affectionate, now partisan and even converted."[14]

There is, therefore, a complex interplay of actions and reactions all along the novel, the weaving of a web of mutual influences that helps the flow of events in its winding march and gives most readers the impression that this long novel is, in fact, not long at all. People listen to each other, sometimes understanding what the other person has to say, sometimes misunderstanding the message: yet they always listen. When, during his first visit to the inn (I, 4), Don Quixote is advised by the innkeeper that no knight should sally forth into the wide world without a good supply of money, clean shirts, and other necessities, the knight takes to heart this good advice. Similarly, Don Quixote's conversation and advice quicken Sancho's mind, make him more alert and even occasionally wise (as we can see during his tenure as Governor of the Island).

Conversation is, therefore, one of Cervantes' ingredients and perhaps the main tool used by him in order to make his characters more flexible and his descriptions more interesting: we can almost say that by and through dialogue the novel achieves unity and even purpose. Dialogue is its essential texture and one of the basic ingredients of its composition. The different proportion of dialogue in the two parts of the novel indicates an important difference between these parts and is further proof of the development of Cervantes' art in the second half of the book.

Dialogue is perhaps Cervantes' greatest artistic discovery—and *Don Quixote* probably the first full-length novel of modern times in which dialogue acquires its greatest depth and complexity. (Let us remember that Plato's *Dialogues* are not novels: their aim and technique are quite different from Cervantes' purpose.) The Spanish critic Dámaso Alonso has pointed out the significance of dialogue in Cervantes' novel by underlining the fact that Cervantes very seldom adds his own comments to what his characters have to say for themselves. It is possible that Cervantes wants to take one or several steps backward, to melt into the background. Possibly, also, he thinks that if his characters know how to express themselves—and they do—anything that the author might add would become superfluous. What Cervantes does is point out the background for his dialogue: where it takes place, the moment of the day, a few descriptions about the position of the people involved in dialogue (what we would call nowadays "body language"). If we compare the style of *Don Quixote's* dialogues with similar pages in Cervantes' *Exemplary Novels*, we come to the conclusion that the art of dialogue in Cervantes reaches its peak in the second half of his novel. The net result is that the novel becomes dramatized: it becomes a medley and an opposition of souls, made transparent to us through dialogue. Américo Castro has emphasized the philosophical as well as the literary intention of dialogue in *Don Quixote:* What is most typical of Cervantes' style is not to attempt the solution of a given problem by applying logic to it (syllogisms were the main tool of the "rationalists" and pseudointellectuals of that period), but rather to attempt to show the projection of a problem in two or more human beings, reflecting their attitudes through a dialogue that does not attempt to be exhaustive nor try to reach a solution. Thus the crucial need for Cervantes to introduce Sancho Panza in his novel: without Sancho, the knight would have to talk to himself. It is curious—and typical—that when Cervantes penned the prologue for the First Part, he decided to invent a friend to speak to—and to get advice from—in order to be able to unfold his ideas, in order to create perspective and depth in his own attitude. We find dialogue, therefore, from the first to the very last pages of the novel. It is in the second part of the novel, when Cervantes knows how to carry out his plans and has perfected his technique, that dialogue reaches its full development: it is also in this second part when the interaction of the two main characters, the knight and his squire, reaches a climax. Sancho Panza becomes increasingly "quixotized" and even at certain moments occupies the center of the stage, having become temporarily the novel's main character. It is an impressive trick: it is not done with mirrors—it is achieved through dialogue.

The traditional purposes of literary innovation have developed along two different yet complementary lines. The first, which can be called technical or artistic, aims at developing new descriptive tools, often by developing at the same time a new sensitivity, new ways of seeing our environment. The second, perhaps most important, by discovering new ways of probing the human psyche and exploring the human condition: this being psychological and philosophical. Only occasionally does a work of art appear in which the technological approach and the philosophical viewpoint are fused: *Don Quixote* is a case in point. Interaction through dialogue leads to a double exploration: the technique of communication unfolds into a clearer knowledge—for the characters in the novel and for the readers outside—of the environment and of the deep self. We realize that the author is not merely interpreting experience; he is attempting to order it both coherently and in relation to his perceptions. He is not merely describing his characters, but investing them with an autonomous life of their own. Cervantes creates Don Quixote, Sancho, and the dozens of secondary characters that give his novel part of its flavor and shape. In turn, Cervantes' own perceptions are changed by this act, in so evident a manner that it is possible to detect the change as the novel unfolds. A god is changed by the world he has created. Like most divinities throughout history, Cervantes keeps making improvements, playing practical jokes on his creation, seeking truth. It is a bold experiment: it can take place through shifts in viewpoint, intermingling of reality and fantasy, ironic changes of fortune, but the most important—perhaps also the most immediately visible—change takes place through the transformation and interaction of psychological characters, especially the interaction between the two main characters, Don Quixote and Sancho.

VI   *The Odd Couple: The Knight and His Squire*

Cervantes has taken pains to create his two main characters as unlike each other, physically and mentally, as possible. The knight is tall, emaciated, a fastidious, well-educated idealist. Sancho is plump, squat, uneducated, practical. Yet they are able to understand each other, they like each other, need each other's company. One of the results of their always being together is the gradual, subtle, and complex transformation of characters which Salvador de Madariaga has called the quixotification of Sancho and the sanchification of Don Quixote. The formula for change is not immediately effective; it is never so completely successful that we cannot see the gulf that still separates the master from his servant. Yet both are drawing nearer each other with each new chapter, each adventure, and each conversation. The formula may be briefly described thus: first Alonso Quijano converts himself—dramatically and suddenly for those who are living in his household, although the process may have gone on for a longer period in the *hidalgo's* mind—into Don Quixote, acquiring thus a new personality and a fixed system of values derived from the romances of chivalry. This transformation, which is described in the first two chapters, is practically complete at the end of Chapter 5. Don Quixote exclaims, "I know who I am!" Turning Sancho into a true believer will take longer. Yet, in spite of Sancho's inborn skepticism and common sense, Don Quixote presses on with his description of the ideal life of a knight-errant and his squire, appealing often to Sancho's obvious weak spot: greed—and love of power. This can be seen clearly in Chapter 21 of Part I. Don Quixote gives Sancho his own interpretation of the adventures that can befall a knight-errant. The account begins in the future tense—later conviction and enthusiasm carry away Don Quixote and he starts using the present tense. What he is describing seems to be happening under our very eyes, under the astonished and approving eyes of Sancho, who feels very much a part of the noble adventures and great successes described by his master.

Don Quixote describes first the difficult early times: ". . . it is necessary for a knight to roam the world in quest of adventures and, so to speak, serve a period of probation, in order that, having brought a number of such adventures to a successful conclusion, he may win such name and fame as will render him well known for his accomplishments by the time he arrives at the court of some great monarch."[15] The knight must be so well known that when he enters the gate of the city all the young lads will follow and surround him, shouting, "There goes the Knight of the Sun," or whatever other name the knight has received. When the knight reaches the king's palace he is discovered to be the son of a king; after several romantic encounters and flirtations, he marries the daughter of the king he serves, and then "the king then dies, the infanta inherits the throne, and, in a couple of words, the knight becomes king";[16] as for the squire, "here is where the bestowal of favors comes in, as he rewards his squire and all those who have assisted him in rising to so exalted a state. He marries his squire to one of the infanta's damsels, undoubtedly the one who was the go-between in his courting of the princess, and who is the daughter of a very great duke."[17] At this point Sancho cannot contain his greed, his hope, his confidence in the rosy future: "That's what I want, and no mistake about it . . . . That's what I'm waiting for. All of this, word for word, is bound to happen to your Grace now that you bear the title Knight of the Mournful Countenance."[18] Words become real for Sancho: he is caught in the same snare that entrapped his master at the very beginning of the novel.

Cervantes understands that the knight's folly, if Don Quixote is left to his own devices, can become destructive, or pathetic, or both. With Sancho at his side, the knight becomes fully human: he shares his projects, his madness, his hopes, with his "sidekick." (It is obvious to any modern reader that the closest parallel to Don Quixote and Sancho in modern times is a "vaudeville couple" with its "funny man" and its "straight man". Yet Cervantes complicates the situation: Don Quixote is not always the one who makes us laugh through his mistakes and his obsessions, often it is Sancho who becomes "funny man" to "straight man" Don Quixote.)

But perhaps, in order to convey the complexity of the relationship between the knight and his squire, we should heed Gerald Brenan's description: "The relationship between the pair may best after all be compared to that most intimate of partnerships, marriage. The long dialogue between them that takes up the principal part of the book suggests, in a more ceremonious key, the familiar dialogue of married couples. It is made up of the same inconclusive wranglings, the same recriminations and *tu quoques*, the same fixed recollections and examples dragged out again and again from the past to clinch an argument. Thus the fact that Sancho was tossed in a blanket early in their travels and that his master failed to rescue him and, to conceal his impotence, put the whole thing down to the work of enchanters, is brought up by the squire every time the question of enchantments is raised in the course of the book. It is one of the two rocks upon which his unbelief, when he is in the unbelieving mood, is founded. Just as in married life, every disagreement leads back to some classic precedent or 'You said so-and-so.' "[19]

This relationship between the two main characters is, with its dialectics of constant disagreements and constant understandings, its point and counterpoint of idealism and sturdy common sense, a principle of organization which prevents the novel from disintegrating into a number of separate episodes. Human memory, the memory of the squire and his master, ruminates upon the past. Imagination and hope work hand in hand to build a future in which both characters will partake of glory. Nothing that occurs in their travels is entirely finished; they will talk about what has happened to them and try to find a meaning to every obscure detail etched in their memory. Every possibility the future holds open will influence their present attitudes. Since the past keeps on echoing upon the present and the future keeps on working its magic upon the minds of the two main characters, each moment of the present is made richer and more subtle by the interplay of past, present, and future.

This interplay is made more plausible—more direct, more poignant—because of the fact that Don Quixote, as a character in a novel, is the first character who lives and grows within the pages of a book; he is never a paragon of virtue or a monster of evil preconceived by a writer and projected onto the printed page. Don Quixote, Sancho, Sansón Carrasco, are both fluid and vulnerable; their thoughts and their actions can be and often are affected by the thoughts and actions of other characters. Occasionally Don Quixote's ideas are Platonic; his actions are rather Aristotelian, inasmuch as an element of pragmatism is often at work in his behavior. Therefore it is not enough to point out that Don Quixote is crazy and that Sancho contracts his master's aberrations, since these disorders are not absolute but relative to the interaction of characters and circumstances. In this manner, their minds are influenced in a fashion that makes them often depart from normal behavior and thus they come to believe themselves capable of carrying out tasks undreamed of in a more sedate atmosphere. The goals these characters try to reach, and often do reach, bring us as readers to a rarefied atmosphere in which both landscape and human figures cannot be seen exactly as before: Something has changed irrevocably because of the inner vision of Cervantes' heroes. The limits of mental weakness and of common sense will hereafter be uncertain and problematical; what before *Don Quixote* had been judged to be an absolute and definable state (to be crazy or to be sound of mind), will now appear to many readers of this strange novel as a condition which affects the functioning of our relationship to other people and circumstances. This is perhaps why Cervantes calls his hero "a complicated madman," "a madman with many normal attitudes."

Obviously Cervantes was building his novel upon a tradition of literary prose works in which absolute values had been presented—and he felt ill at ease within this tradition. He had to create his novel "from scratch," inasmuch as his characters were going to receive from him a freedom and an ambiguity that had been impossible to achieve in most previous novels. This need for freedom brought him to create around his characters what we may call "breathable atmosphere," depth, perspective. His characters stand out as rounded figures, not as linear projections upon a canvas; around them there is space enough so that they can move in many directions.

Perspective is often created by the many opinions which his characters are bound to express when judging one single event: we come very often upon sentences like "he thought it to be so, and (somebody else) thought otherwise." Through the underlining of such differences of opinion, the act of seizing and understanding reality becomes in a way subjective: reality is incorporated into the being of each speaker. This does not mean that Cervantes is bringing us into a philosophical discussion. There is nothing abstract in the nuances of reality perceived by each character, but rather the interaction between the individual and his environment is shown to be unique: it escapes logic and language because logic and language are systems of labels superimposed upon our experience, and Cervantes wants to free us from all labels by showing how each individual is capable of interpreting his own facet of a multifaceted reality. No general conclusion is drawn by the characters or by the author: they are all too busy being alive, walking, talking, riding—and, in the case of the author, too busy describing his characters' actions—to take the time necessary for general conclusions. (Let us notice in passing that the environment in Cervantes' novel is strictly rural, with the only exception of one brief visit to Barcelona; it is more spontaneous and more fresh, perhaps more naive, than the environment favored by philosophers, who, from Socrates to Descartes, always preferred the city to the countryside.)

The characters' inner freedom, their apparently limitless capacity for autonomous development, means above all that the current stereotypes, both social and cultural, had to be shattered. Sancho, for instance, should have been a practical, crafty, materialistic peasant from the first page to the last; yet here and there—most noticeably when the artificial power is vested in him by the dukes during the days in which he is the ruler of the Island—he rises to a much higher level; he becomes a wise ruler, almost a statesman, a country moral philosopher. This level, however, cannot be sustained forever; Sancho is bound to fall back upon his selfish and crafty ways. Yet the boundless possibilities of even a humble man without any formal education have appeared tantalizingly in a few pages of Cervantes' novel.

Sancho and Don Quixote, Don Quixote and Sancho: all the interest of the novel seems to concentrate upon the two main characters, to the point that when they are absent from the action, during the interludes provided by the novelettes, our attention may wander; and when one of them alone occupies the center of the stage, we are anxious to know what the other is thinking, how he is going to react to the adventures of his friend. Obviously, therefore, Sancho is one of the pivots of the novel, as essential for the well-being of Don Quixote as—on a loftier plane—the image of his beloved Dulcinea.

VII *Don Quixote in Love*

One of several paradoxes in *Don Quixote,* perhaps the most obvious, is that the most important character after Don Quixote and Sancho, a character whose presence and influence are constantly felt, is Dulcinea, a character created entirely by the imagination of Don Quixote. Let us observe in passing that Don Quixote, as a personality, has been created by the imagination of Alonso Quijano, and that we hear about the whole process through the complicated device of a manuscript written in Arabic by a Moorish historian (and as the readers of Cervantes' novel well knew, Arab and Moorish historians in general were considered in Golden Age Spain to be inveterate liars). Dulcinea is a ghost in the mind of another ghost. Her unreality is what we might call a "second-degree unreality"—yet her influence cannot be denied. In order to understand her importance, we must remember that Don Quixote is always ready to model his behavior, his system of values, his emotional attitudes, upon those of his favorite knight-errant, Amadís of Gaul—and Amadís was hopelessly in love with the beautiful Oriana. How could Don Quixote aspire to become a first-rate knight-errant if he had no lady to give his love to? A lady had to be created in a hurry to make our hero more plausible, more complete, more perfect. Only by comparing Dulcinea with her counterpart, Oriana, can we appreciate the originality of Cervantes' novel.

Amadís de Gaula (Amadís of Gaul) is perhaps the most famous of all Spanish romances of chivalry. Its modern version was written by Garci Rodríguez de Montalvo, a contemporary of Ferdinand and Isabella; dates of his birth and death are not known. His book was published in Saragossa in 1508. It is based upon an older text whose author is unknown and that seems to go back to the second half of the fourteenth century. Its action takes place in England: therefore "Gaul" should be read here as "Wales." An offshoot of the Arthurian legends, it is bathed in the pale light of medieval platonism. The hero, Amadís, is the prototype of knightly perfection, moving in a mysterious atmosphere and always protected by supernatural forces, guided by the wisdom of a white witch, Urganda. The plot unfolds in a series of battles against monsters and giants, yet violence never carries the reader too far from spectacular moments of magic, spells, love potions, miraculous recoveries, and also tender love scenes: courtly love can become at times explicitly erotic. Amadís, the natural son of King Perion of Wales and his beloved Elisena, is cast adrift at birth in a boat. He carries with him a ring and a sword. He grows up in the home of Gandales, in Scotland, as a son. Later on, as an adolescent, he visits the court of King Languines, where he meets Oriana, daughter of Lisuarte, king of Brittany. It is love at first sight. Their first kiss reminds us of Lancelot and Guinevere—and unavoidably of the adventures of our Prince Valiant of comic strip fame. They swear to be faithful to each other for life. Through Oriana's intervention, Amadís is dubbed a knight; he goes forth in search of adventure with Oriana's beautiful image always present in his heart. The novel is basically and typically medieval: love plays an important role and is a magical, complete fulfillment, carrying the lovers beyond reality to a realm of absolute liberty where they may act without any restrictions. For Amadís his beloved lady is like a bright lodestar who guides him along the pathways of sacrifice on to honor and glory. With its conception of love and its dream of liberty and justice, *Amadís* managed to reflect perfectly the high ideals of chivalry of the late medieval and early Renaissance period: for this reason it enjoyed an immense popularity, becoming the favorite reading of kings and emperors: Francis I and Charles V among others, as well as philosophers like Montaigne and writers like Bembo and Castiglione. The love of Oriana and Amadís—and this is a point in which Cervantes will not follow the early novel—is not completely abstract and platonic. On the contrary, it is based in large part on a mutual physical attraction. Amadís falls in love with Oriana immediately upon seeing her for the first time. In the novel's third book they even have an illegitimate child, a fact which they must conceal for a long time because of the existence of a law which condemns to death any woman who has sexual relations out of wedlock. Therefore we may say that the love between Amadís and Oriana is not a "perfect" love according to Christian ethics and the socially accepted morality, but the two lovers do carry to the highest possibilities the virtue of loyalty: Amadís can therefore win the contest of the Magic Arch of Loyal Lovers—a man who has been unfaithful to his loved one can never cross this magic threshold—and is then rewarded by being made the ruler of an Island.

It is worthwhile to emphasize that Amadís attributes all his physical and moral strength to his love for Oriana. There is a direct relationship between prowess on the battlefield and the beautiful image of the lady that the knight carries in his memory like a glorious flag. This is why the relationship between Don Quixote and Dulcinea, which in principle should be the same close, loving, strength-giving relationship, turns out to be pathetically—and comically—different. Don Quixote has never seen Dulcinea: he has simply drawn in his imagination an idealized portrait, which surpasses in beauty and virtue Helen of Troy, the Latin chaste and beautiful Lucretia, and any other famous woman of antiquity. Obviously, the creation of this paragon has some practical uses. For instance, during one of his visits to the inn, the maid Maritornes, who is trying to keep an amorous appointment with one of the muleteers who, together with Don Quixote and Sancho, are spending the night at the inn, wanders by mistake into the arms of Don Quixote. The knight is old and tired—he has received a beating a short time ago—yet his imagination runs riot: "Forcing her to sit down upon the bed, he began fingering her nightgown, and although it was of sackcloth, it impressed him as being of the finest and flimsiest silken gauze. On her wrists she wore some glass beads, but to him they gave off the gleam of Oriental pearls . . ."[20] He holds tight the terrified girl, who during all this time has not said a word, and then, after calling her "beauteous and highborn lady" and explaining that he is bruised and tired, he adds that the reason why he cannot respond to her advances is "my word and promise given to the peerlesss Dulcinea del Toboso, the one and only lady of my most secret thoughts." The excuse seems to work—Maritornes keeps struggling in silence to get away, finally the muleteer senses what has happened, comes close in the dark and stuns the knight with a blow to his jaw. The scene is full of comic tension—and also pathos: we begin to assume that Don Quixote's experience with women has been extremely limited and all his love affairs have been platonic.

Dulcinea is to Oriana what Don Quixote is to Amadís: this formula helps us understand why the knight of La Mancha needs Dulcinea, needs to believe in her beauty, and has to have his lady's beauty accepted and proclaimed by all those who cross his path. Yet he may be aware that his lady exists only in his mind—and that even this precarious existence is constantly menaced: Dulcinea will be enchanted by the magicians who pursue Don Quixote; she will be turned into a coarse peasant girl. This fact is a heavy burden to carry: the whole second part of the novel is made more tense, more pathetic in spots, by this hovering ghost of the enchanted Dulcinea, since we know that when the lady has lost her beauty, how can the strength and valor of her beloved survive for long? Don Quixote's self-doubts will be increased considerably when he realizes that, try as he will, he cannot erase from his memory the last image of Dulcinea, the enchanted Dulcinea with her donkey, her coarse language, her poor looks.

Every scene of the novel where Dulcinea is influential—more yet, every scene where Don Quixote is involved in any way with Dulcinea or any other woman within a framework of sensuality, eroticism, love—turns out to be among the funniest in the whole book. Don Quixote is thus defined by his creator as a sort of Amadís with bad luck. He never takes his beloved in his arms, never makes love to her, the help that her image should give his arm is often nonexistent, almost always insufficient to win the battle; moreover, if Don Quixote has chosen to model himself upon Amadís, he is bound to remember that Amadís was young, strong, and handsome, while he is old and no longer strong; that Amadís was always protected by a "good fairy," a white witch, while the enchanters that pursue Don Quixote have never performed any good deed. On the contrary, they keep playing dirty tricks upon him. Only then we realize that the fortitude necessary for the knight to go on from one adventure to the next, for such a long time, without losing hope completely, is almost superhuman. His fidelity to Dulcinea, to her memory and her love, is also nothing short of miraculous: It is born at the very beginning of the novel, at a moment when Dulcinea has a real-life model and has not yet become the ethereal creature known only to Don Quixote. We read in Chapter 1 that "as the story goes, there was a good-looking farm girl who lived near by, with whom he had once been smitten, although it is generally believed that she never knew or suspected it. Her name was Aldonza Lorenzo, and it seemed to him that she was the one upon whom he should bestow the title of mistress of his thoughts. For her he wished a name that would not be incongruous with his own and that would convey the suggestion of a princess or a great lady; and, accordingly, he resolved to call her 'Dulcinea del Toboso,' she being a native of that place. A musical name to his ears, out of the ordinary and significant . . ."[21]

Don Quixote superimposes upon the vague memory of a country lass all his ideals about perfect feminine beauty and distinction: he falls in love with the music of the word, "Dulcinea" and his platonic conception of feminine beauty rather than with the farm girl of his memory. Years after *Don Quixote* was written, a perceptive nineteenth-century French writer, Stendhal, would describe the phenomenon of falling in love as a "cristallization" or superimposition of images and ideals upon a human being to whom one is attracted. Don Quixote's creation of Dulcinea is such an extreme and radical phenomenon of "cristallization" that the knight can dispense with the existence of a real human being: Aldonza Lorenzo will never be seen again by Don Quixote, she may have died for all we know (and he knows), yet Dulcinea exists for him in all her splendor. It is the last reality to vanish in his mind; when she fades away, at the very end of the novel, when he realizes that she cannot be disenchanted, he accepts his failure as a knight-errant at the very same time. He heads for home, to become again Alonso Quijano—and to die.

The death of a hero, even a would-be hero, is a serious matter, and in this case the serenity that descends upon the dying man cannot make us forget the pathos of his grief a few hours before, when the absence of Dulcinea and his own repeated failures compel him to abandon all his plans and all his hopes. Dulcinea is thus associated with the emotional highlight—failure, despair, pathos—at the end of the novel; yet often she plays a role in the comic highlights, especially the episode of the Enchanted Dulcinea (Chaper 10 of Part II).

This incident is especially amusing and original because in it the roles of Don Quixote and Sancho are reversed. Until this moment it was the knight who, through his feverish imagination and his literary memories, was able to transform humble facts of everyday life (an inn, some windmills, etc.) into fabulous visions worthy of the best romances of chivalry; Sancho resisted, warned, criticized, appealed to the knight's common sense. But the knight had sent messages to Dulcinea through Sancho, and Sancho, unable to find the lady, had lied and pretended he had in fact delivered his master's letter; he is now being asked to find the palace where she dwells, for Don Quixote wants to pay her a visit. He is embarrassed and feels guilty: he decides to deceive his master. He waits outside the hamlet for a while, thus making Don Quixote believe that he has in fact found the palace and will now bring his master to her. Sancho sees three peasant women riding donkeys towards them: he hurries to his master's side and announces that Dulcinea and two of her ladies-in-waiting are coming to greet Don Quixote. Sancho describes their beauty and splendid dress with great gusto: yet Don Quixote this time can see nothing but the drab reality.

The quixotization of Sancho is here—for the purposes of his little dramatic act of deception, his practical joke—all but complete: his descriptions are worthy of the best romance of chivalry, he is eloquent and precise, and insists that in fact the peasant girl on the donkey is Dulcinea; his master, subdued, kneels in front of the girl; the donkey rears, the girl falls, curses him, remounts in grotesque haste, and gallops away. Don Quixote is overwhelmed, downcast, almost in despair. He seizes upon a solution: Dulcinea has been enchanted, her real self transformed and hidden from his view. It is the old story of "The Emperor's Clothes"—but the sad knight cannot and will not accept that what he has seen is the naked truth.

The episode is so carefully planned and executed by Cervantes' art that the reader is compelled to laugh from the beginning to the end of it. Cervantes contrasts Sancho's pompous language, a language that he has acquired from his contact with the knight, as Sancho has had no formal education, with the progressively coarser language of the girls. Every moment and every expression of the characters are described at the right moment: rhythm and timing are flawless. It is an episode such as this one, by no means exceptional in its comic quality, yet perfectly effective, that allows us to understand how much the art of Cervantes owes to the theatre. All the elements of a good farce—misunderstanding, confusion, deception, fast dialogue, contrast, grotesque movements, surprise, even a hint of violence—are present. It is not in vain that Cervantes had spent countless hours writing plays: he loved the stage and would again write excellent plays after finishing Part I of his novel. The stage had taught him how to handle fast dialogue, how characters should move, how to end a scene. It had taught him, above all, how to handle the elements of farce.

Yet if only theatrical elements were present in this and other comic highlights of the novel, it is hard to see how *Don Quixote* could have achieved its permanent success as an international classic. There is always more than meets the eye in its pages. Specifically, beneath the veneer of farce, parody, and laughter there are philosophical problems about appearance and reality, truth and illusion, subjective fantasy and objective knowledge. These are at bottom intellectual problems. Other problems, connected with personality and psychological adjustment to society, are also very much in the background, ready to be deciphered by the reader if he is interested. Farce is effective as a comic expression of human shortcomings—yet it is seldom subtle. What Cervantes achieves is even harder than writing a good comic scene: the philosophical and psychological underpinnings are always present, giving each scene a greater depth. Don Quixote used to believe in Dulcinea as completely and uncritically as a believer accepts his God. Suddenly the mysteries of amorous faith are shattered when the believer wants to check empirically the existence of his beloved. What was real in his imagination seems to have left the visible world—if it ever existed there—and taken refuge in Sancho's inner vision: no wonder Don Quixote is increasingly confused. His psychological attitudes are also revealed: he is capable of imagining monsters, giants, castles—yet his powers of imagination are not infinite; he may be caught off-guard, too tired or too confused—or too emotionally involved—to be capable of rejecting the description given by Sancho. In short, he can be manipulated. Usually it is the knight who imposes his vision upon others: they are either overwhelmed by his attitude or, as Erich Auerbach points out, "they humor him in his *idée fixe* in order to get some fun from it. The innkeeper and the whores at the time of his first departure react in this way. The same thing happens again later with the company at the second inn, with the priest and the barber, Dorotea and Don Fernando, and even Maritornes. Some of these, it is true, mean to use their game as a way of getting the knight safely back home, but they carry it much farther than their practical purpose would require. In Part II the *bachiller* Sansón Carrasco bases his therapeutic plan on playing along with Don Quixote's *idée fixe;* later, at the Duke's palace and in Barcelona, his madness is methodically exploited as a pastime, so that hardly any of his adventures are genuine; they are simply staged; that is, they have been especially prepared to suit the *hidalgo's* madness, for the amusement of those who get them up."[22]

We see now clearly that Don Quixote is both exalted and imprisoned by his identification with Amadís, and the parallel identification of an obscure country lass turned into Dulcinea with Oriana, Amadís' beloved: the identification as a source of strength is much in evidence during the first part of the novel, since it gives the would-be knight-errant the mental energy to fashion his life around his new self-conception—and the physical energy to undertake strenuous adventures and to rebound from serious physical mishaps. Yet imagination is contagious, as Sancho demonstrates with his "recreation" of Dulcinea; two can play at the game. In the second part of the novel especially, Don Quixote will encounter with increasing frequency secondary characters who are already alerted to his special brand of folly because they have read the first part of the novel: they can thus play the game much better, they can anticipate and manipulate the *hidalgo's* reactions: once more literature and life appear inextricably mingled.

VIII   *Literature and Life in* Don Quixote

Most modern readers would react, if told that a novel contains allusions to other works of fiction and even whole passages devoted to literary criticism, by thinking that the novel in question is probably a pedantic work, a boring and bookish tract of limited interest, appealing at most to graduate students in literature. Yet this description fits *Don Quixote.* I do not mean to suggest that Cervantes' novel is pedantic or bookish. On the contrary, it is fresh, down-to-earth, and makes fun of pedantry. Yet it is impossible to deal with it without realizing that many of the materials from which it is built come from literature. Its very conception is based upon a synthesis (not a compromise) of two different subgenres of fiction: the romances of chivalry and the picaresque novels.

A romance, it has been pointed out by Northrop Frye, is a peculiar type of fiction that appears usually at the end of a historic era, embodying in exaggerated form most of its values. Its idealization and the fact that it deals with old-fashioned attitudes makes it into escape literature. *Don Quixote* as a novel bears an ambiguous relationship to the romances of chivalry in general and *Amadís* in particular. As a parody it pokes fun at them. Yet the creation of its main character, Don Quixote, out of a poor bored *hidalgo*, Alonso Quijano, and the vast amounts of psychic and physical energy released by this creation (made possible by the existence of ideals embodied in the romances of chivalry) attest that for all practical purposes these ideals have not disappeared altogether. The romances of chivalry may be bad literature, as several characters in *Don Quixote* will point out carefully. Their adventures may be farfetched and outrageously out of touch with logic, common sense, everyday experience. (Cervantes, whose tastes were often curiously old-fashioned, must have enjoyed reading them in the same fashion that a serious critic today may decide to spend a weekend reading a James Bond novel: he knows it to be artificial, contrived, unreal, yet it will make his weekend more pleasant.) Yet what other model of prose fiction could be opposed to these romances? Only the picaresque novel. Cervantes knew and appreciated picaresque literature, yet he had certain reservations. Allusions to the romances of chivalry are numerous in *Don Quixote*, especially in the chapter describing the scrutiny of the *hidalgo's* library (I, 6). Less attention is paid to picaresque novels. Yet when Don Quixote liberates the galley slaves (I, 22) he asks one of them, Ginés de Pasamonte, about Ginés' autobiography: " 'It is so good,' " replied Ginés, " 'that it will cast into the shade *Lazarillo de Tormes* and all others of that sort that have been or will be written. What I would tell you is that it deals with facts, and facts are so interesting and amusing that no lies could equal them.' " [23] The adventures of Ginés de Pasamonte resemble the exploits of Guzmán de Alfarache, the hero of Mateo Alemán's picaresque novel, who writes his life in a galley, where he has been forced to row as a consequence of the delinquent acts he has committed, much more than they do Lazarillo's. Obviously Don Quixote prefers the romances of chivalry to the new genre, the picaresque novel, which is alluded to by Ginés de Pasamonte. What are Cervantes' preferences? As usual, we cannot be completely certain: Cervantes lets his characters express their viewpoints without intervening in the debate: he is more a Master of Ceremonies or a moderator in a round-table discussion than a speaker with a clear thesis. As Claudio Guillén puts it, "a dialogue in Cervantes is a joining of critical perspectives, and it would be impossible for him to embrace fully either the technical simplicity of Don Quixote, as far as the narrator's craft is concerned, or Ginés de Pasamonte's allegiance to the picaresque form."[24]

Of course, Cervantes' reservations towards the romances of chivalry are more apparent, and he states specifically, as an author-critic, in his preface, that his novel will try to destroy the influence of such books. And yet we are faced with criticism of a peculiar nature. As E. C. Riley has observed, "the critique of the novels of chivalry is made in two ways: by more or less direct judgments within the fiction, and also *as* the fiction. Criticism in fictional form is conventionally parody, and to some extent the *Quixote* is parody, but it is unusual in containing the object of the parody within itself, as a vital ingredient. The novels of chivalry exist in the book in just the same way as Rocinante or the barber's basin. They are so palpably present that some of them can be burnt. Cervantes' originality lies not in parodying them himself (or only incidentally), but in making the mad Knight parody them involuntarily in his efforts to bring them, by means of imitation, literally to life."[25]

As for the other prose genre, or rather subgenre, the picaresque, it is also present in *Don Quixote*, and we find traces of it in almost every chapter. We should not forget that Cervantes wanted to paint in his novel a microcosm of Spanish society—and in his Spain the underworld, the oppressed masses, whatever label we choose to give to the picaresque elements in society, could not be ignored: it was present everywhere, a mixture of cynicism, charm, and anguish. Cervantes knew this aspect of Spanish life well: he had been poor, he had been in jail, he had lived in the capital of Spanish picaresque life, Seville. Yet it is significant that the most picaresque of the characters in Cervantes' novel, Ginés de Pasamonte, seems to criticize the picaresque novels by implying that they are not faithful enough to reality—and also that they do not tell the whole truth; they lie. Besides which, he refuses to say how long his autobiography is going to be: it is fully planned, but it is not finished; when asked whether it is finished, he answers, "How can it be, when my life is not finished yet?" (I, 22). Ginés de Pasamonte is the embodiment of picaresque novels; he is the picaresque novel come to life—yet he seems to criticize the genre inasmuch as he claims this sort of novel is too rigid, not truthful enough, not to be compared with the spontaneity and freshness of true human experience.

The picaresque genre is basically alien to Cervantes. There is no dialogue in it, almost no real human contact, a vision of reality devoid of even a trace of idealism, a constant insistence upon the limitations of man's strength and vision, an acute loneliness. How could Cervantes accept its principles? The picaresque novel sees the world through the eyes of one single frightened individual. Cervantes, master of dialogue and perspective, had to find his literary path elsewhere. As Carlos Blanco Aguinaga aptly describes the picaresque genre, "the picaroon is a lone wanderer, a true exile who never achieves authentic dialogue with other men because most of them distrust him and he distrusts them all, once he has acquired a little experience. And though he deals with everyone and everyone deals with him, all the diverse attitudes of others are filtered to the reader through his loneness, and at the center of his loneness reality, however prismatic, becomes fixed in a single point of view from which, by its very lowness of perspective, the falsity of other points of view is exposed. Because of this single point of view, the loneness of the picaroon results in total isolation from the hostile world and thereby justifies itself: in this isolation the picaroon finds his superiority over the rest of mankind, and from this superiority he drives his basis for judging and condemning them."[26] Let us also remember that Mateo Alemán, the great writer who had turned his *Guzmán de Alfarache* into a bestseller, must have loomed in Cervantes' mind as a dangerous rival for the favors of the reading public. It is in fact Cervantes' success with *Don Quixote* that made the novel by Mateo Alemán less interesting to the Spanish readers: after Cervantes' book appeared, the success of *Guzmán de Alfarache* came to an almost abrupt end. At any rate, Cervantes' hero, a man of vision and lofty ideals, was the antithesis of the picaroon: yet the picaresque mode is present in the environment of the knight, in several secondary characters (Ginés de Pasamonte, the lowly characters at the inn). There is no literature in the life of a picaroon: the life of Don Quixote is full of literature. It is motivated by literature and acquires its full dimension by trying to make literature come alive: Don Quixote wants to fulfill his existence as a true "work of art."

It should not surprise us. In this respect Cervantes' character is much more typical of the Renaissance (or, in any case, of the official and accepted view of man during the Renaissance, what we might call the "ideal" or the "facade" of the Renaissance) than any picaroon. Freedom, the dignity of man, the need to live one's life as a work of art, were paramount principles in Renaissance thought. Baldassare Castiglione (1478-1529)) had published his famous treatise, *Il Cortigiano (The Courtier)*, in 1528. Cervantes was familiar with it. In its four dialogues Castiglione had defined the perfect gentleman, with a well-balanced education, good manners, always serene and cool, elegant and refined, versed in the sports, the use of weapons, music, the arts, literature—and Platonic love. The perfect gentleman's life was a true work of art. The mind and the body reached in him a perfect balance. The eloquent speech by Don Quixote on the subject of Arms and Letters (I, 38) echoes this need for both types of exercise and the respect due to both (Don Quixote is as much a frustrated writer as Cervantes was a frustrated warrior). Don Quixote, therefore, bends his will to the effort: he will try to turn every moment of his life into a work of art. Of course, the spirit is willing—but the flesh is weak. He wants to become poetry and ends up as parody. He has trouble distinguishing between reality and fiction. According to Aristotle, the artist must imitate nature. Don Quixote could have imitated nature and become a writer; he imitates fiction and turns his life into subfiction, parody, because he cannot reach his true goal. Reality is too intractable, his strength fails him. He is not the only one to fail at this demanding task. A famous book of his times, *The Imitation of Christ*, encouraged the devout to shape their lives by following a book, the Gospels. How many succeeded in this task? How many Tartuffes for each true mystic?

The power of books over a man's life is therefore the constant theme of Cervantes' novel, a serious undercurrent giving depth to the clownish pranks and the farcical events that fill its pages with merriment. When we realize how much men's lives have been changed by the power of books, whether the Bible or Mao's Little Red Book, whether the Homeric epics inspiring Alexander the Great to his endless conquests, or the romantic romances that troubled Madame Bovary, we come to the conclusion that literature and our daily lives are like two distorted and shifting mirrors placed in front of each other. Each change of perspective, each shift in the mirrors, opens up new vistas and compels us to new actions.

The power of literature is especially strong on Don Quixote because it is obvious from the very beginning of the novel that he is a true intellectual. Who else but an intellectual could have sold the land his ancestors had left him in order to buy books? In this respect he stands much closer to his creator, Cervantes, than to the *hidalgo* social class he is supposed to represent: few *hidalgos* could boast of Don Quixote's library, of his culture, his poetic imagination, his memory for literary facts. Don Quixote takes great pains with words, with language—the hallmark of a poet. He chooses his own name, the name of his horse, the name of his lady, with exquisite care: he knows that names do matter, that, in a way, they are or can be the essence of the person, object, or action they stand for. He knows the rules of rhetoric: how to organize a sentence, a speech, a description. His vocabulary is uncommonly large, another sure sign of his intellectual vocation. His memory is excellent: he knows by heart long poems, ballads, quotations. He suffers quite often from an affliction that has been the bane of more than one writer. He misjudges his audience, he overestimates the culture and understanding of those he addresses, hence a communications gap which produces embarrassing and comic effects: his courtly remarks to the prostitutes at the inn and his well-balanced speeches to the goatherds fall on deaf (and confused) ears. When Sancho is about to become the ruler of the Island, he receives from his master a wise lesson on moral and social behavior that compares favorably with Polonius' advice to Hamlet.

Don Quixote composes poetry on occasion. He is capable of imitating the old-fashioned language of the romances of chivalry. Finally, this vast effort at creating a new self and a life that conforms to the rules of art gives Cervantes' main character a considerable charm: Don Quixote is a free man, one of the few men that have ever existed. He makes full use of his *libre albedrío*, his free will, and this is one of the sources of his happiness. For there can be no doubt about it: during almost all of the first part of the novel, Don Quixote is a happy man. He never had so much fun when he was simply a lonely bored *hidalgo*. It is by an act of will that his personality was created, by repeated efforts of free will that he endeavors to turn his life into a work of art—and almost succeeds. Here and there there are moments of rest, reflection, contemplation, in which Don

Quixote could undo what he has done, go back to his primitive self. He refuses to do so. Happiness is contagious: obviously Sancho, who claims to be a practical man, becomes infected by his master's inner satisfaction and is in turn happier than ever before. Otherwise it is hard to explain why he should continue to follow Don Quixote, neglecting his family and his land, when the salary he receives is meager or nonexistent and the hardships keep raining upon his shoulders. The breath of the air of freedom, the knowledge that each one of them is fashioning his own life not according to tradition or routine, but rather by following the dictates of his heart and—especially in the case of Don Quixote—by becoming a poetic being, a novel-turned-into-man, is what sustains the couple in the most dangerous and painful adventures.

It has been said with respect to a contemporary of Cervantes, Lope de Vega, that he never knew where his own private life ended and where fiction, his own fiction, the fiction into which he put so much of his own experience, began. This is also true of Cervantes' main character. For him life must be as beautiful and fulfilling as literature; literature must lend itself to the daily needs of human life. Needless to say, this confusion is at the source of endless practical problems for the knight and his squire. The situation is made more complicated because Cervantes is not satisfied with creating problems for Don Quixote. He is going to present the readers of his novel with three pairs of antithetical ideas or currents, which he uses throughout the book as a way of organizing his materials: the opposition madness-sanity, obvious when we notice certain aspects of Don Quixote's behavior; the opposition art-reality, which is also apparent in the behavior of our knight and the way this behavior—which assumes both art and reality are part of one and the same thing—is judged by his contemporaries; and finally, the opposition between subjective-objective, or between appearance and reality, which leads us into the realm of philosophy.

As Robert Alter has pointed out, one way of understanding how the modern novel was created is to view the novel, or rather the history of the novel, as a dialectic between consciousness and things, between personality and the world of stubborn, inert, and unyielding objects that surrounds each personality. This tension between man and his surroundings is perfectly understood by Cervantes. It is unknown to the novelists and prose writers that preceded him. There is no dialectic of this sort in the older narrative forms because they generally reflect a sense of organic connection between man and the things around him. In a society basically untroubled by social and ideological conflict, there is an unconscious acceptance of our surroundings: we feel at home, our objects—our clothes, our tools, our homes—prolong and extend our personality. We do not have to fight them in order to become ourselves. They are a help, not a hindrance. Often certain objects, like Achilles' shield described by Homer, are sacred, fashioned by a god, or linked with a glorious past. Yet since the Renaissance, this sense of organic connection between man and things has broken down. The process of alienation, so often mentioned by Hegel, Marx, and Marcuse, is far advanced in the modern world. It was already present when Alonso Quijano decided to become Don Quixote and tried to fight the gray inert quality of the objects that surrounded him: "his heroism consists in his brave, pathetic, noble, and of course mad attempt to force the indifferent things of his world into consonance with his own heroic ideals—basins into helmets, windmills into dragons, broken-winded nags into fiery steeds."[27]

This tense interplay between the knight and his environment is one of the keys to Cervantes' success and enduring influence. In a dynamic world such as ours, the classical works we understand and like best are those that embody tension and drama. Of course, it is worth asking why Don Quixote goes mad. Cervantes states that "his brain dried up," which is a short description related probably to the theory of humors—four humors the balance or imbalance of which would determine good or bad health in the human body—as described by the Spanish physician and psychologist Huarte de San Juan in his *Examen de Ingenios.*[28] This explanation is also a dialectic one: in the struggle for supremacy, one of the humors in the human body displaces its opposite humor and takes over. Hence, an imbalance and lack of good health. There is a similar imbalance between the *hidalgo* and his society, between Alonso Quijano and his environment. The *hidalgo* in general feels frustrated, alienated, superfluous: this is very much the case of Cervantes' character. Obviously there is more in the opposition between health and disease, common sense and madness, as seen and presented by Cervantes, than meets the eye: we shall see later that Cervantes' novel is not devoid of social criticism. It is true that Don Quixote takes leave of his normal society, tries to change it and perhaps subvert it in the name of an old-fashioned ideal. Yet what alternatives did his society offer him? Was the pattern of oppression and corruption worth saving? Cervantes' answers to these questions are not crystal-clear, nor could they be, given the temper of his times, given an intellectual climate that included censorship and the Inquisition. Yet the answers are there if we care to look for them.

IX   *Cervantes' Shifting Mirrors*

What is the borderline between art and reality? Art, we know, is or should be, according to Aristotle, a mirror to reality, an imitation of reality. Inasmuch as "realistic" art is thus closely linked to reality, it should not indulge in excessive flights of imagination which might break the connection with the real world. Thus Cervantes, at certain moments in which Don Quixote's fantasy seems to go too far, takes care to warn us that it is impossible to vouch for the authenticity or verisimilitude of the knight's descriptions. A case in point is the curious dream or vision of Don Quixote at the cave of Montesinos. Yet the novel offers us layer upon layer of "relative reality," of reality more and more distant from believable everyday reality. It is a tale, a fiction, and we know its author is Cervantes; yet he claims he is conveying to us the interpretation of Benengeli, a ridiculous name for a Moorish historian who is perhaps a liar. Many critics, among them Ortega y Gasset, E. C. Riley, and myself, have underlined the role of perspective in Cervantes' tale. Perspective had been rediscovered by Renaissance artists and mathematicians: it afforded a precise description of the visible world from one viewpoint; it shifted and changed with each movement of this viewpoint, hence its subjective nature, yet it gave a good description of the world as seen by one observer. Cervantes uses several perspectives, according to each character. Riley puts it this way: "The *Quixote* is a novel of multiple perspectives. Cervantes observes the world he creates from the viewpoints of characters and reader as well as author. It is as though he were playing a game with mirrors, or prisms. By a kind of process of refraction he adds—or creates the illusion of adding—an extra dimension to the novel. He foreshadows the technique of modern novelists whereby the action is seen through the eyes of one or more of the personages involved . . . "[29]

The reader seems to be faced with a Chinese nest of boxes, or a

Russian Easter egg, or an onion with layer upon layer of "reality." Cervantes pretends that his fiction is history. Into this history several kinds of tales are inserted. Some of these tales, the story of Marcela and Grisóstomo among others, belong to the literary genre of the pastoral romance. Others remind us, as does the tale of the *Curioso impertinente (Idle Curiosity)*, of Italian short stories: we have thus the "story-within-the-story" and also, with Pedro the Puppet Master (II, 25-26), the "play-within-the-play," as in *Hamlet*. When knight and squire meet a cart full of actors and actresses fully dressed in their theatrical costumes (II, 11), we are again in a dream world. Is not all the world a stage?

The sense of unreality is heightened throughout Part II when Don Quixote and Sancho have to face their doubles, their reflection in the mirror. They meet people who have read Part I or have heard about it; they have to react to what these readers of their previous adventures think about them. Even worse: After II, 36, they have to fight off another image of themselves—the bogus image in the crooked mirror of Avellaneda's fake Second Part, the False Quixote. Towards the end of July, 1614, Cervantes was working on Chapter 36 of his second part; Avellaneda's book appeared in October of the same year. Cervantes reacted by writing thirty-eight chapters in seven months: a strenuous effort which may have exhausted what was left of a precarious health. The spurious second part was the work of an unknown author, but Cervantes' hard-won reputation was in danger until he could refute the piracy by issuing his own Part Two. He was also indignant at the lack of intelligence and sensitivity of his imitator. His anger is expressed through his main characters. Don Quixote and Sancho have to face their ugly ghosts: they must convince the readers of Avellaneda's book that *they* are real and Avellaneda's characters are intruders trying to usurp their personality, their selves, their reality. It is a situation only Cervantes or Pirandello could have devised.

It is not surprising therefore that poor Don Quixote is unable to ascertain what is true and what happens only in his imagination: "everything that our adventurer thought, saw or imagined seemed to him to be done and to happen in the manner of the things he had read" (I, 2). Modern readers are not much better off. They keep wondering about the role of Cervantes in this complicated stage set. He places here and there discrete clues pointing toward himself (as in the tale of the Captive, I, 39-41) which make us aware that Cervantes is at the same time outside of his novel, manipulating cleverly the unseen strings, and inside it, very much like a modern film director who not only creates a film, but also appears briefly in it as one of the most obscure secondary characters. Most of the time Cervantes stays back, aloof, from his characters, allowing them as much freedom as they can acquire. When he does interfere with the action, he does it in a spectacular way. In Chapter 8 of the First Part, Don Quixote and the Biscayan are engaged in mortal combat: we can almost see them facing each other with their swords raised, ready to strike. Suddenly, Cervantes tells us, the manuscript ends: we are left holding our breath, in the height of suspense. The moving images have become frozen, we are forced to wait until Cervantes finds the missing pages of Benengeli's manuscript. We realize that Cervantes, not satisfied with playing tricks on his heroes, is pulling his reader's leg. Suspense had perhaps never been carried to such heights.

Our sense of having to deal with several kinds of "reality" is nowhere so strong as when the adventures of Don Quixote and Sancho are interrupted to make way for one of the interpolated short stories, "those tales," as Leo Spitzer puts it, "which, far from imitating the genre of the main plot, precipitate us into an atmosphere of romantic nowhereness, where the laws of realism have ceased to exist, and where imagination alone holds sway."[30] These novelettes have always puzzled Cervantes' critics. If the author was trying to destroy the influence of romances of chivalry, why should he let into his novel by the back door all these tales written in an unrealistic mood which reminds us of the romances? Leo Spitzer gives a plausible solution to this enigma: "The whole of the Cervantine novel falls then into two parts: the one teaches criticism before imaginative beauty, the other re-establishes imaginative beauty in the face of all possible scepticism. But since the illusionistic stories are interpolated into the critical novel (not the reverse) and since they are found only in the first part of the novel, we must assume that Cervantes, while desiring to counterbalance the corrosive effects of the anti-novel by the admixture of traditional illusion, did not hesitate to subordinate the older approach to the new: with him criticism is victorious in the century of Descartes—even in Spain."[31]

To penetrate into the never-never land of some of these tales after a robust and funny dialogue between Don Quixote and Sancho is like a lightning-fast trip between a wooded hill and the top of Himalaya. Obviously Cervantes thought that a world totally dominated by an atmosphere of realism would be poor indeed. It is true that idealism ruled unchallenged in some of the recesses of Don Quixote's mind. Yet idealism had to be accommodated in some of the nooks and crannies of Cervantes' novel. It made for better balance and also gave greater relief to the bulk of realistic scenes in the novel. Cervantes does not want to draw in black and white: he likes shadings, hues, gradations of light and color. By introducing scenes that lack in realism, he underlines much more strongly, by contrast, the realistic sections. Even language (specifically, the vocabulary in the speeches of each character) is helpful to create an illusion of depth. The knight's vocabulary is full of historical terms and archaic words: it turns our attention to the past. The goatherds or the enchanted "Dulcinea" speak with the coarse language of illiterate peasants living in a present with limited horizons. Many other characters help to establish a full spectrum. What appears to be a barber's basin to some spectators will be seen as a glorious golden helmet by others—and perhaps other witnesses will reach a definition of this object entirely different from the other two interpretations. Sancho offers a compromise: Why not call this object a "basin-helmet"? Perspectivism in language, as Spitzer has shown, is one of the most curious and significant stylistic traits of the novel. Cervantes knows only God is in possession of ultimate truth; it is not for mortals to pretend absolutes can be reached. Therefore, one should not be in a hurry to judge other men's behavior; it is utter folly to lay claim to the ultimate meaning of reality. As a good leader of a discussion group, Cervantes allows each character to have his say.

X *Cervantes as a Social Critic*

We may well suspect that although the author has been extremely polite with the characters he has created, giving them leisure to develop their personalities—to the point that they seem to acquire a life of their own and develop into "autonomous characters"—he would also like, occasionally and in an unobtrusive way, to communicate to us his ideas and feelings; there may be a message hidden in his novel. This message, if indeed it exists, has been hidden carefully, or at least not exposed for all to see. Cervantes' contemporaries seem to have paid scant attention to it. Cervantes, excluded from the intellectual élite of his time, a shabby-genteel middle-class *hidalgo* at odds with the law, was probably not anxious to hoist to a mast each and every one of his opinions and beliefs. He was more interested in creating a novel where freedom of beliefs could have full range. The hovering presence of censorship and the Inquisition should not be underestimated. More socially secure, conservative, and orthodox writers such as Francisco de Quevedo and Baltasar Gracián would come in conflict with the Establishment and suffer keenly as a consequence. Cervantes was not anxious to become a martyr. No wonder that we have to read between the lines if we are to find anything in his novel that resembles social criticism.

And yet, we feel, it is there—if we look for it. Some of this criticism seems to be directed primarily to the middle class. It should not surprise us: we can criticize only what we know best. Cervantes was familiar with the shortcomings of daily life as lived by the middle class. Criticism, like charity, should begin at home.

Some sociologists and historians have cast doubt about the very existence of a Spanish middle class during the Renaissance and the seventeenth century. Cervantes knew better. He made his hero a member of this class, to which he himself belonged. It was a class with limited horizons and an uncertain role, yet it existed. It was made up of poor *hidalgos*, petty State employees, not a few "New Christians," i.e., converted Jews. It was perhaps the group that bought most books and read them avidly, as if to find in books a wider horizon, an escape hatch from a dungeon. Cervantes' message to this group, as well as to all Spaniards, is simple: "Do not believe everything you read." Try to distinguish between dreams and reality. A critical novel was needed, Cervantes thought, in order to warn fools that took literally the fantastic world of romances. Printing had made literature available to masses of people previously limited to a restricted diet of sermons and oral ballads: intoxication with literature could become a form of mental alcoholism. A century before Cervantes, Rabelais had extolled the virtues of the printed word. Gutenberg had become the father to a bookish generation that was fast losing touch with reality.

The printed word, it was becoming obvious, was a two-edged weapon, a dispenser of knowledge and folly. A correction was overdue. Reason and common sense, as well as long experience, were needed in order to separate the grain from the chaff. The reading of obsolete books can become an obstacle to progress. We must bear in mind that Cervantes' message, perhaps the most explicit message in his novel, with respect to the dangers of interpreting literally the romantic world of the romances of chivalry, is not as simple and "innocent" as it may seem. It is indeed simple and innocent if we take it at face value: "mistrust fantastic, unrealistic literature; treat it as a diversion, not as a guide in daily life." The situation changes if we generalize: "mistrust any literal interpretation of the printed word, since there are many paths to truth, and none is sure; avoid blind acceptance of dogma, use your critical reason." The path leads then to Descartes and the Enlightenment. Cervantes wrote before the Thirty Years' War had ravaged Europe because of certain literal and conflicting interpretations of sacred texts given by opposing nations and groups; yet the spectacle of religious wars was not unfamiliar to him. Was the larger message implicit in his restricted message? In all probability we shall never know.

If we compare Cervantes' mind to a pianist's keyboard, we come to the conclusion that the right hand is playing a dominant melody—and this melody speaks to us about criticism, common sense, reason, the need to control what we read, what we feel, what we think. Yet the left hand plays about beauty, illusion, dreams. The counterpoint of poetry and fantasy is needed, Cervantes thought, so that our world does not become too practical, rational, ultimately dry. He did not, and could not, turn against poetry and imagination: only against its abuses. Yet for a *hidalgo* trapped in a sterile environment, they were his only escape.

For in fact the *hidalgo* class was trapped. A *hidalgo* could not work in commerce or industry: nobility was a barrier to most lucrative endeavors, yet the land owned by most *hidalgos* was too poor to yield a decent income. Obtaining employment in the government or the royal entourage required contacts, allies, friends: Many *hidalgos* had none. Military service, Cervantes knew it well, was a dubious escape. It led to glory, sometimes, more often to a prison camp, where the soldier would languish for years; even liberation was often a way back to a country where the soldier's merit would be forgotten. War had become a way of life—yet it proved no solution to the problems of Europe. Don Quixote, or rather Alonso Quijano before becoming Don Quixote, was doubly trapped: as a *hidalgo* he could not earn a decent living; as a first-born (let us remember he has a niece, therefore some brother or sister), he could not leave the land, he had to stay at home and take care of the ancestral home and holdings. No wonder he dreamed of escape.

Not all of Cervantes' critics would agree that his novel contains elements of social criticism. Marxist critics are of course in the foreground of the effort to discover Cervantes as a social critic. In some cases the interpretations seem farfetched: Thus the Italian writer Giovanni Papini, in *Don Chisciotte dell'Inganno* (Don Quixote the Deceiful), 1916, advanced the theory that the knight feigned to be mad so that he could mock the world around him with full freedom. It is evident that Cervantes did not write a simple book; new interpretations of *Don Quixote* are always possible, yet Papini's is impossible to accept because it goes against a number of explicit statements by Cervantes. One-sided points of view are seldom tenable.

If indeed Cervantes is a social critic, what are his targets? The whole *hidalgo* class could be said to have been the victim of Cervantes' mockery. Yet the *hidalgos* were only part of a complex social system: they were not entirely responsible for their predicament. It was a system of values that downgraded honest work, made it suspect and unworthy of a nobleman, that was chiefly responsible for the decadence of the petty nobility.

Yet once more it is not easy to be perfectly sure about Cervantes' targets. Cervantes has been called "sly,", "slippery," "hard to pin down," when it comes to social criticism. We do know that several of his minor works, especially his short stories, such as *The Deceitful Marriage* and *The Dogs' Colloquy*, express a didactic meaning easier to define than the critical meaning present in *Don Quixote*. Cervantes knew and accepted Horace's dictum about mixing the useful and the pleasant in a literary work, and we should be able to read his message. Unfortunately, most critics cannot find a consensus about this message. Yet it seems relatively clear that part of this message can be related to Cervantes' criticism of the Spanish class system, another part (even harder to define) to the ideology of his times. The social criticism in Cervantes' novel is never as clear as in the chapters where (in Part II) Don Quixote and Sancho spend some time in the Duke's palace. This is a topsy-turvy world: the Duke and the

Duchess are real nobility, exalted aristocrats. Don Quixote is a mad *hidalgo*, his squire an ignorant peasant. Yet it is Don Quixote and Sancho that outshine the aristocrats. Life at the palace is revealed by the duenna to be petty, devoid of real affection and love, lacking in high goals. The only purpose of the aristocrats is to have fun at the expenses of Don Quixote and Sancho, playing on them elaborate jokes that border on cruelty. Don Quixote with his elegant speeches and wise counsels to Sancho, and especially Sancho with his impeccable behavior as Governor of the Island, are the true aristocrats, noble in heart and mind; the Duke and his wife are unmasked as shallow, frivolous, empty-headed.

Similarly, Cervantes will show us innumerable examples of social cruelty and excessive use of official authority. A boy is being whipped by his master in I, 4: the fifteen-year-old boy has been tied to a tree and Don Quixote cannot stand this unfair punishment to one who cannot defend himself. The excuse given by the boy's employer is baseless and callous: "this lad that I am punishing here is my servant; he tends a flock of sheep which I have in these parts and he is so careless that every day one of them shows up missing. And when I punish him for his carelessness or his roguery, he says it is just because I am a miser and do not want to pay him the wages that I owe him . . ."[32] The truth happens to be that he does not want to pay the boy and finds it cheaper to punish him instead. Don Quixote's efforts to right the wrong prove counterproductive—yet the reader has been impressed from the very beginning of the novel with the cruelty and injustice of Cervantes' society.

The chapter in which Don Quixote frees "many unfortunate ones who, much against their will, were being taken where they did not wish to go" (a curious roundabout way to define convicts, galley slaves) is also significant. In it the knight places himself squarely on the side of freedom. Why should the government turn anyone into a slave? Anyhow, Don Quixote says, the penalties meted out to these poor people are too stiff (and indeed they are, especially for a modern observer: Don Quixote is here way ahead of his times). It does not matter that Don Quixote spoils the whole relationship by insisting that the convicts should pay a visit to Dulcinea: once more it turns out that Hell is paved with good intentions—yet the critical point with respect to Spain's penal system has been made and remains impressed upon the reader. Even the interpolated tales may have didactic meanings. The story of the shepherdess Marcela (I, 13-14), who refuses to fall in love with Grisóstomo just because he has fallen in love with her, strikes a blow for women's independence and freedom: Cervantes turns out to be one of the first feminists of his time. The episode of Camacho's wedding (II, 20-21) seems harmless enough at first reading. An old rich man, Camacho, is about to wed a young girl. Yet she loves penniless Basilio. Love makes people clever; they devise an ingenious trick whereby her wedding takes place—to unite her and Basilio. It is all very amusing until the reader starts to think about the fate of the girl, practically sold by her parents to the rich man, if the trick had not succeeded. A somber aspect of Spanish social life emerges, a sad and cruel situation in which the young had very few rights and a girl was practically owned by her parents until she could be married off to the highest bidder.

Other aspects of Cervantes as a critic, as we have pointed out before, are harder to ascertain. Was Cervantes a follower of Erasmus, who had tried to breach the gap between Catholics and Protestants and preached an "inner religiosity" almost devoid of external ceremonies? Cervantes seems to make fun of the Church in one or two passages. He involves the Curate with the inquisitorial burning of books (I, 6), has the knight fashion a ridiculous rosary (I, 25), makes the Curate laughable by having him "put on the disguise of a wandering damsel" (I, 26-27), and on the occasion of Don Quixote's visit to Dulcinea (II, 9) has him pronounce the fateful phrase, *con la iglesia hemos topado* ("It is the church we've lighted on"), and then associates the church and the churchyard (death). Much has been read into these brief sentences by some critics; their interpretations have been disdainfully dismissed, in turn, by other critics who point out instead the many passages in which Cervantes' orthodoxy shines. Was Cervantes an anticlerical, a liberal, a reactionary? We know he was cautious in his criticism—and why should he not have been cautious?—yet on the whole he must have been anti-Establishment, he was critical of the King (at a time when few Spaniards dared to be), and there were many aspects of Spanish society that he probably disliked. It is significant that he seems to have been happier in Italy than in Spain and that in one of his *Exemplary Novels* he praises almost without reservations England's Queen Elizabeth I (almost continually at war with the Spanish crown). Cervantes knew by direct experience how profound the crisis of Spanish society was: yet his criticism of it is veiled by laughter. It is the comic spirit in the novel that was immediately accessible to Cervantes' contemporaries; later, the romantic readers would uncover a tragic side to the knight's endeavors. They would see in Don Quixote a hero in search of true greatness, summing up all the longings to destroy lies and conventions, usurped dignity, and superannuated ideologies, whose aim was to destroy so as to rebuild on the bodies of the defeated giants a world in which there would be ample scope for love, truth, and poetry. The tragedy is that Don Quixote failed in his task. Yet we are left with a vital and anguished protest against the obtuseness of the majority.

Don Quixote may have failed at the herculean task of rebuilding his society: he managed at the very least to establish in his own mind, and perhaps also in the mind of his readers, the legitimacy of dreams and of protest. It is undeniably true that we would seek in vain for a precise conclusion, a moral to the fable. The fact that many messages, often contradictory, have been found, seems to prove that we can approach Cervantes' meaning only "through a glass, darkly." No precise solution emerges from these dreams and these protests. Lord Byron thought that Cervantes' novel had sounded the death knell for the Spanish heroic spirit and therefore had accelerated the political decadence of Spain. The authors of the modern musical comedy, *Man of La Mancha,* on the contrary, believe that the enthusiasm and idealism of the knight are infectious: Sancho and Dulcinea, somehow, will continue the struggle and the quest. Obviously, when a novel can give birth to diametrically opposed interpretations, we cannot be sure that its message is clear and universally accepted. Cervantes may have explored every major avenue in his efforts to rediscover man and put him together again from the distorted fragments and fantastic dreams that constitute his hero. But alchemy often fails, in any case the recipe Cervantes used in order to create his hero cannot be easily deciphered. Don Quixote's death puts an end to the quest: it is true that the knight mutates again, becomes the *hidalgo* of the first pages of Part I, dies a serene, wise, and Christian death; yet his death, which seems to contradict the very spirit of Don Quixote, comes perhaps because the knight is exhausted, his enemies are too numerous; this does not mean that his quest was useless, only that it was impossible for him to achieve victory. He often spoke of his enemies in terms of giants, dragons, evil enchanters. We should know better: they should be named hypocrisy, mediocrity, lack of imagination, obtuseness, greed, cruelty, despotism.

XI *Towards a Philosophy?*

The Spanish philosopher Miguel de Unamuno used to say that Spanish philosophy had to be sought in literature, for the most part in writers like Cervantes and the mystics. It is evident that Cervantes' pages may suggest problems related to human reality, the meaning of life, and man's role in the world. Was Cervantes fully conscious of the philosophical significance of some of his pages? It is typical of his art not to offer us any clear-cut theories, and also not to offer us one-sided moral speeches after the fashion of many of the writers of his time, such as Mateo Alemán (this may be one reason why his novels seem to be, and indeed are, so different from the picaresque works). Cervantes simply relates the facts and allows the reader to draw his own conclusions.

For Cervantes, indeed, offers no solutions. As Angel del Río has stated, "what emerges from the *Quixote* and to a lesser degree from his other works (a few of the *Exemplary Novels*, some of the *Interludes*) is that our world, our life, is above all ambiguous. That certainty is not possible, that the world is susceptible of many interpretations."[33] The man of Cervantes' period, which is to say the man of post-Renaissance and Baroque times, sees existence often as a game: at times a tragic game, others a comic game; but the game is based upon an interplay of contradictions. In the seventeenth century, the rationalistic attitude appears to gain the upper hand in many European circles, thanks to the efforts of a Descartes and a Spinoza, among others. Their rationalism grew out of doubt, yet it proclaimed the supremacy of reason: Man's rational thought should be the only criterion of truth in a world that was organized along geometric lines and general ideas. The classical French heros (as, for instance, the heroes and heroines of Corneille and Racine) are reasoners in the field of morality: they analyze their feelings endlessly, establish a clear system of values, finally act accordingly. Calderón's characters are also great analysts and know how to argue—within the prescribed limits of Catholic scholasticism.

One might almost say that all the great writers of the Baroque period have studied law and Scholastic logic, and as a result many of their characters reason impeccably. Law and logic are clear, as clear and precise as the differences betwen black and white. Cervantes is not at all inclined to this attitude. Before literature acquired the rationalist and argumentative bend of the mature Baroque period, both Shakespeare and Cervantes, each in his own way, and each without any knowledge of the other, had already come to grips with the anguished problem of being and nothingness. They describe a world in which man does not know how to distinguish clearly between truth and the appearance of truth, that is to say, the image of truth that he himself fashions. Man is impelled by his own passions, illusions, feelings, appetites. He is a reasoning animal only occasionally, not always successfully. Many tragic moments of the English dramatist are based upon this fact: Man is not wholly—perhaps not really—rational. Love and hatred are always more powerful than a perfect syllogism. Shakespeare generally grants knowledge of the greatest and deepest truths to characters devoid of high education and unsteeped in logic and science: to his buffoons and fools, while his dramatic heroes, even if they know better, succumb to their passions. Something similar may be said to occur in the Spanish comedy (of Lope de Vega, for instance) in the contrast between the knight and his servant (the *gracioso,* or comic valet, who so often sees the world in more practical and precise terms than his master). In the theatre, the truth enounced by the fools and buffoons is often what we might call "everyday practical reality," a practical code to cope with the world as is, to cope with a crisis, in contrast with fantasy and rhetorical self-deception as practiced by gentlemen. "Cervantes goes still farther," Angel del Río states, "because he juxtaposes and finally partially fuses ideal truth, created by Don Quixote's faith, with the pragmatic truth of Sancho, and in the subtle game of truths and illusions, of madness and of common sense, he permits us to see how the squire becomes more and more like his master while his master begins to accept in the course of his disenchantment Sancho's vision."[34]

The fact is that we both admire Don Quixote and laugh at him. We admire his courage and his idealism, we cannot but laugh at the meager results of his efforts. He seems to fail in the everyday world; yet we know that his example is a glorious one—we need it in order to go beyond our limited horizon.

The Spanish writers who came after Cervantes, such as Quevedo, Calderón, and Gracián, emphasized the unreal characteristics of our earthly existence in order to place in front of it, or rather above and beyond it, the world of eternal truth, light, and glory, the Christian Heavens. Only the right behavior, the correct morality, seen within an orthodox framework, can give us a passport to the Heavens and eternal salvation. There is often a tone of intellectual and religious propaganda in Baroque Counter-Reformation literature that is not entirely in agreement with our contemporary taste. Cervantes is much more subtle and approaches every human problem obliquely, ironically. What is the point of acting, of trying to change the world, he seems to tell us. On the other hand, if we dare nothing, imagine nothing, we shall become as dull as some of the characters around Don Quixote, ever ready to criticize the knight, incapable of understanding his ideals. Wrapping his thought in ambiguities is perhaps one of Cervantes' most fortunate solutions: as an artist, a poet, an analyst of the human heart and its passions, Cervantes did not even try to give us solutions, which would have been beyond his scope; rather he wanted to present human life in all its richness, its ripeness, its constant contradictions. As Tennessee Williams in his most successful recreation of the Don Quixote myth, *Camino Real*, has the knight say, "Life is an unanswered question, but let's still believe in the dignity and importance of the question."[35] Cervantes could not have put it better. Perhaps Tennessee Williams' sentence expresses succinctly the message of Cervantes' great novel.

XII   *Some Highlights*

An enumeration of the adventures of Don Quixote and Sancho along the many chapters of the novel would be useless to those readers who know the book well—and insufficient to those who do not. Let us instead describe briefly some of the highlights of the novel, relating them to some of the general characteristics of the book described previously. The first chapter describes Alonso Quijano, the "lean-bodied, thin-faced" *hidalgo*, and his passion for the romances of chivalry. After losing his wits he decides to become a knight-errant. He patches up as best he can a rusting suit of armor that had belonged to his great-grandfather and, after christening himself Don Quixote, his nag Rocinante, and the "lady of his fancies" Dulcinea del Toboso, goes forth in search of adventure (I, 2).

He is ready to meet giants and sorcerers—less ready for the banality of things around him. Nothing but heat and space for a whole day. He arrives at night at a modest lodging for mule drivers—and his fancy projects upon the mediocre surroundings the noble and elegant world where he would like to live. Instead of an inn, he sees a castle with turrets, moat, drawbridge, and pinnacles of silver; the two prostitutes loitering in the doorway of the inn are for him two high-born ladies (he will address them in an ornate, sophisticated, and old-fashioned language that they will be incapable of understanding); a swineherd who blows a sort of whistle to gather his hogs will be for him the herald announcing his arrival to the lord of the manor. He is served moldy bread and poorly cooked codfish—but thinks he is eating biscuits and trout. When he tries to eat and drink, he finds that he cannot unfasten his visor nor take off his helmet. He is trapped inside his armor: "It was a mirth-provoking sight to see him eat, for he still had his helmet on with his visor fastened, which made it impossible for him to put anything into his mouth with his hands, and so it was necessary for one of the girls to feed him. As for giving him anything to drink, that would have been out of the question if the innkeeper had not hollowed out a reed, placing one end in Don Quixote's mouth while through the other end he poured the wine" (I, 2). This is only the first of many "mechanical mishaps." As Henri Bergson, the French philosopher, has observed, and Cervantes well knew, the prevalence of a mechanism over a human endeavor is always a good source of humor and laughter. The people at the inn perceive the knight's madness and decide to humor him: the innkeeper pretends to be the lord of the castle, and when Don Quixote asks to be dubbed a knight by him he grants his request with exaggerated pomp and mock dignity; one of the prostitutes girds the knight's sword while the other buckles his spurs; they can hardly keep from laughing behind his back.

In I, 4, he is on the road again, tries to right a wrong (a boy is being whipped by his master), and succeeds only in making things worse for the boy, who is whipped again as soon as Don Quixote leaves the scene. The knight then meets some merchants on the road, takes them for knights-errant and orders them to praise aloud the beauty and virtue of the peerless Dulcinea. They refuse; a fight ensues; they give him a severe thrashing. A fellow villager finds him lying unconscious on the road and takes him home. But Don Quixote is stubborn: he will go out again, this time after convincing a peasant, Sancho Panza, to accompany him as his squire. He promises him riches, fame, the governorship of an Island—and Sancho comes along mounted on his donkey (I, 7). Meantime his neighbors, the Curate and the Barber, sensing that Don Quixote's folly springs from his reading materials, go over his library and burn most of his books.

Chapter 8 deals with the adventure of the windmills. Once more Don Quixote's imagination tampers with reality. He imagines the windmills to be giants, charges one of them, is caught in the sail, is lifted and tossed down by it. Sancho had objected. Yes, the *hidalgo* admits, it is indeed the sail of a windmill: only because the magician, Frestón, has turned the giants into windmills in order to frustrate him. The defense mechanism is at work: the knight will attribute to the magician's wicked intervention every mistake and misadventure that befalls him.

Chapter 9 deals with the fight with the Biscayan—a fight that Cervantes "freezes" with the swords in midair because, he claims, he has run out of manuscript. Chapters 14 and 15 are an example of ironic contrast. In Chapter 14 we are still in the romantic and somewhat unreal world of shepherds and shepherdesses: Grisóstomo loves Marcela, is not loved in return, commits suicide. Chapter 15 tells us how Rocinante "falls in love" with some mares, pursues them, is beaten by the mule drivers that own the mares. Don Quixote attacks them in spite of Sancho's timidity: "How the devil can we take revenge, when there are more than twenty, and we are only two—or perhaps no more than one and a half?" Don Quixote replies, "I am equal to a hundred." The battle ends badly for our heroes. That, says the knight, serves him right: he should not fight people who are not dubbed knights. Somehow he has to find an explanation for every mishap. They make their way into another inn —another castle according to Don Quixote—and during the night the scullery maid Maritornes mistakenly comes to the knight's bed (she had agreed to spend the night with a muleteer whose bed was close to Don Quixote's) and is courteously rejected by the knight, whose love for Dulcinea prevents him from loving any other "lady." The jealous muleteer attacks him in the dark. A wild brawl ensues between Don Quixote, the muleteer, Sancho, the girl, the innkeeper who comes to the rescue (I, 17). The castle, Don Quixote concludes, is enchanted.

On the road once again, they encounter a barber who is travelling and, since it is raining, is protecting his head with his basin, made of yellow metal. Don Quixote, convinced it is the miraculous helmet worn by the legendary pagan king Mambrino in Ariosto's poem, *Orlando Furioso,* attacks the barber and takes over his "helmet." The object does indeed look like a barber's basin to most dispassionate witnesses. As the knight explains to Sancho, there is a crew of enchanters always amongst them who change and alter all their deeds, and transform them according to their pleasure and their desire either to favor one or injure him. So what seems to Sancho to be a barber's basin appears to Don Quixote to be Mambrino's helmet, and to another as something else.

At the foot of a tall mountain in the Sierra Morena, in Andalusia, Don Quixote decides to rest. He will make penance, since he has not heard from his lady and thinks he has been forsaken. He will wait there while Sancho delivers a love letter to Dulcinea and returns with her answer. Sancho departs, only to run into two old friends of his master, the curate and the barber. They are coming to lead the knight back to his home, and hopefully to sanity. Everybody in the village is worried about him. They convince Dorotea, a girl who is travelling in order to find her vanished lover, to help them: she will disguise herself as "a damsel in distress," Princess Micomicona, and the barber, disguised with a false beard, becomes her squire. Back to Don Quixote they go, and Princess Micomicona implores the knight to defend her against the traitor who has usurped her kingdom: the road to her country goes through the inn—and through Don Quixote's village; they expect thus to bring him home. But the barber's false beard falls off. Everybody invents false explanations, makes speeches, acts or overacts. Most characters seem to be crazier than Don Quixote, who has become especially serene and dignified. He is convinced that he is setting out on a memorable undertaking. But the innkeeper makes a mistake: he lodges Don Quixote in a room full of huge skins of red wine. The knight dreams that he is battling 'he giant who has usurped Princess Micomicona's throne—and as if in a trance, he splits the wineskins open with his sword. The torrents of spilled "blood" bring more confusion and recrimination. We can best define some of these chapters by saying that they remind us of a historical film acted out by the Marx Brothers.

After a few more hallucinations and soliloquies, and in order to avoid further surprises, Don Quixote is placed, together with Sancho, in a large wooden cage, which is transported on an oxcart. He is told that he is under a magic spell and he lets himself be transported back to his village. Thus ends Part One. We must, however, remember two points: the chapters in which action takes place are only about one-third of the total; another third is made up of the reflective chapters: dialogue, speeches by Don Quixote, and another third by the interpolated novelettes, of which the most interesting one is the "Story of the One Who Was Too Curious for His Own Good" (Chapters 33, 34, 35), a curious tale about a self-fulfilling prophesy. A man who is obsessed by the idea that his wife may someday be unfaithful to him, decides to put her through a test by having a friend of his make advances to her. The husband goes away, his friend performs his task only too well, and, as we might have expected, the young married woman weakens: "Camila surrendered, yes, Camila fell. Was it to be wondered at if friendship in Lotario's case could not keep its footing? Here we have an example which shows us clearly that the passion of love is to be conquered only by fleeing it. There is none may grapple with so powerful an enemy, for divine strength is needed to subdue its human power" (I, 33). Beware of obsessions, Cervantes seems to tell us.

Part II opens with Don Quixote ill in bed. His housekeeper and his niece are doing their best to keep him comfortable and happy—to no avail. After a month of enforced idleness, our knight is back on horseback and faithful Sancho is once more with him. They are bound for El Toboso, where Don Quixote hopes to see Dulcinea. Sancho is supposed to know where she lives, but of course does not. He finds a way out: he will point out a peasant girl to his master and describe her as Dulcinea. The roles are reversed: it is Sancho who describes a beautiful damsel— and Don Quixote who is unable to see her (II, 10). Dulcinea, the knight concludes, has been enchanted. "I can see nothing," he complains, "but three village girls on three donkeys." He falls on his knees before the enchanted Dulcinea, bemoaning his sad fate. He must liberate Dulcinea from the enchantment, perhaps offering her the gift of a great victory over a giant or a knight. Soon afterwards (Chapters 12—14), he is in fact challenged to a duel by a mysterious knight. This is no other than the Bachelor Sansón Carrasco, whose stratagem is simple: he will defeat Don Quixote and then compel his defeated enemy to obey him, according to the laws of chivalry, and then he will order Don Quixote to go back home and forget his dreams. Ironically he fails: although older and weaker, Don Quixote wins the battle and goes on his way.

New adventures await him. He defies a caged lion by opening the cage (Chapter 17), but the lion is either sleepy or tired, and merely turns its posterior on Don Quixote. Chapters 20 and 21 deal with wealthy Camacho's frustrated wedding. Afterwards Don Quixote explores the mysterious and deep Cave of Montesinos. It is perhaps a parody of Aeneas' descent into Hell. In any case, the knight probably falls asleep inside the deep cave and, upon coming back to the surface of the earth, tells Sancho about his strange and grotesque visions. A knight's heart is paraded by a group of strange damsels: upon his death he had bequeathed it to his lady, and since they are not sure of finding her right away, they have had it salted, as if it were a salami. Dulcinea wants to pawn her petticoat to Don Quixote, if only he will give her half a dozen coins. It is obvious that Don Quixote's subconscious mind is being revealed in these visions, a subconscious mind full of doubts and unable to turn to real poetry the fragments of memory and his previous dreams which have become for the most part broken, fragmented by the constant battering of everyday reality. Later on the knight and his squire arrive at the palace of a real Duke, where they are the butt of endless jokes. Sancho proves to be more popular and successful: he is granted by the Duke the governorship of an Island. His dream has come true. For a few days, and with the help of his master's advice, he rules with wisdom and benevolence, only to be deposed by a mock invasion. The last adventures are even sadder: Don Quixote is unhorsed by the Knight of the White Moon (again Sansón Carrasco in disguise), and the latter imposes upon him a hard sentence: he must give up knight-errantry for one year and return to the village.

He returns, downcast and distressed, suffering from a fever. After a long and deep slumber, he awakens cured of his madness: he recovers his wits only to die. He makes his last confession to his friend the curate and takes leave of this world serenely, as a Christian gentleman, abjuring his errors and his madness. His existence as Don Quixote depended on his being able to believe in his dream; he had to die as soon as he found himself once more in the presence of concrete reality.

The second part of the novel more than fulfills the promise of the first part. We are no longer distracted by interpolated tales. Sancho's character comes to full bloom—and his personality occasionally outshines that of Don Quixote. The dialogue is wittier and funnier. The tale comes full circle back to earth, to normalcy—and death. A double emotion, a mixture of melancholy and resignation, pervades these last pages of Cervantes' masterpiece.

CHAPTER 8

Cervantes' Swan Song:
Persiles and Sigismunda

I Cervantes' Favorite Novel

I T seems probable that *Persiles and Sigismunda,* Cervantes' last novel, was his favorite work. It is certain that he never invested as much care and love in the composition of any of his other works. In his opinion, or at least he so states towards the end of his life, this novel was the most perfect of all In his dedication to the Count of Lemos, which appears in the second part of *Don Quixote,* referring to *Persiles,* which he thought at that time he would finish within four months, he states: ". . . I myself now take my leave by offering Your Excellency *The Trials of Persiles and Sigismunda, . . .* It ought to be the worst or the best that has been written in our language—I am referring, of course, to books designed for entertainment. As a matter of fact, I repent having said 'the worst,' for according to the opinion of my friends it should be extremely good." [1]

Persiles was published in Madrid in 1617, one year after Cervantes' death. Its last pages seem to have been finished hurriedly. Its author, who had built such illusions about this novel, must have felt anguished about the idea of dying without putting the finishing touches on it, and worked with feverish intensity during the last months of his life. The fourth book of *Persiles* consists of only fourteen chapters, compared with the twenty-three, twenty-two and twenty-one of the other books or sections. Moreover, these last chapters are much shorter then the rest. This fact and some examples of carelessness of style in a work otherwise so scrupulously written lead us to believe that perhaps Cervantes was unable to revise these pages.

This novel was published by Cervantes' widow in Madrid in 1617, as we have stated, and in the same year by several other publishers in Valencia, Barcelona, Pamplona, and Brussels. Probably Cervantes had begun writing it at the same time as the second part of *Don Quixote*. He finished it a few days before dying. In his dedication to the Count of Lemos he states poignantly, "There is an old song, once famous, which begins, 'Having placed my foot in the stirrup.' I wish its words did not fit so closely my own predicament, since I can now use almost these very words:

> *Puesto ya el pie en el estrivo*
> *Con las ansias de la muerte,*
> *Gran señor, esta te escrivo.*
>
> (*Having placed my foot in the stirrup,*
> *A prey to the agony of death,*
> *Great Lord, this I write to you.*)

Yesterday they gave me extreme unction, and today I write you these lines; time is short, my agony grows, hopes diminish. And in spite of all this, I keep alive because of my desire to go on living . . ."[2]

With this novel, therefore, Cervantes takes leave of life and of glory, and the farewell of its preface reminds us of the death of Don Quixote.

The complete title of the novel is *The Trials of Persiles and Sigismunda, a Northern Adventure*. The words "Northern Adventure" better describe the first two books of the novel, which are set in the foggy Nordic shores. It is a Northern Europe described with all the fantasy of the Baroque period. *Persiles* could be described as a romance and a novel of adventures, a "thriller for lovers." Its situations are based on the usual pair of lovers upon whom Fate visits the most unexpected trials and dangers, but who must finally win; the book ends with the happy union of the lovers. Cervantes makes these situations, which the Byzantine novels had already explored, fit a more modern era, conferring upon his couple all possible poetic and Christian virtues, and substituting for the bright Mediterranean world the shadowy Northern one.

The plot is not too hard to follow. Persiles, the prince of Thule, and Sigismunda, the daughter of the king of Friesland, pretending to be brother and sister under the false names of Periandro and Auristela, journey through the vast seas and lands of Europe, starting from the faraway frozen Northern shores near the pole, going south by sea and land, crossing Portugal, France, and Italy until they reach Rome. They must obtain from the Pope a blessing for their love, a love which emerges chaste and pure from the most terrible trials and adventures. The complicated plan of the novel, which is based on a main narrative line that is frequently interrupted, permits the author to suggest the constant intervention of a blind fate under whose mysterious and capricious influence the characters look for happiness only to be frustrated time and time again.

The first two sections of this novel are developed by Cervantes along the lines of a wild succession of adventures: shipwrecks, kidnappings, separations, dreams, premonitions. It is a dream world, similar often to the dream world of Shakespeare's *The Tempest*, a world of unreality, ghosts, constant doubts about the reality of everyday life, a world in which, like Calderón's Segismundo in *Life is a Dream*, we are never quite sure whether we are awake or dreaming. Periandro, for example, narrates a splendid vision full of color and delight in which he saw emerald meadows, fruits of every kind, precious stones, in a setting of mild skies, a splendid procession of chariots and allegorical figures, and he states, "I broke the dream and the beautiful vision disappeared," and when asked, "Then you were dreaming?" "Yes," he replies, "since everything good that happens to me turns out to be a dream."

Persiles turns out to be a huge book of adventures, a poetic novel of chivalry, which rights the failure of the hero in *Don Quixote*. It is of unequal interest with respect to its plot and its development, yet nevertheless is written in a style which is perhaps the richest in nuances, most elegant and terse Cervantes ever employed.

II   *A Poetic Synthesis*

Everything Cervantes knew about poetry, rhythm, harmony in language can be found in the pages of *Persiles:* some of his sentences truly contain "the sound of music." The novel is, as the Italian critic Arturo Farinelli puts it, "Cervantes' last romantic dream." It unites the two aesthetic criteria applied by Cervantes to his own works: idealization and realism. The idealization is here much more visible, it dominates the whole novel, yet from time to time we can also find sentences, sayings, observations, which remind us of *The Glass Scholar* and other *Exemplary Novels.* This is especially true of the second half of *Persiles,* Books 3 and 4, where we leave behind the mysterious Northern shores and come down to the bright world of Mediterranean sunlight. Cervantes knows his surroundings much better: he had invented every detail in his descriptions of Northern Europe; he can now rely on his experience and his memory, and perspicacious observations reappear at this moment. As soon as he brings his characters to the squares and towns of the contemporary world, he regains his true nature as a humorist and a keen observer of human nature, human foibles, local color.

Cervantes' novel is also a geographic synthesis, a recapitulation of everything the author knew, directly or indirectly, about Europe, its lands, its mountains, rivers, seas, inhabitants, and customs. To be sure, we are not dealing with a scientific treatise: on the contrary, Cervantes takes great liberties with geography as we understand it today. We must take into account the fact that the books on this subject available to Cervantes were, on the whole, closer in style and accuracy to Marco Polo's famous description of his trip to the Orient than to our modern maps and the descriptions of the *National Geographic Magazine.*

Accuracy in geographic details was certainly not among the virtues of the great writers of this period. Two examples shall suffice. In *The Tempest,* Shakespeare assumes that Milan is either a seaport or is situated very close to the sea. Thus, when Prospero narrates his sad story to Miranda, he states:

> The King of Naples, being an enemy
> To me inveterate, hearkens my brother's suit;
> . . . .
> A treacherous army levied, one midnight
> Fated to the purpose, did Antonio open
> The gates of Milan; and, i' the dead of darkness,
> The ministers for the purpose hurried thence
> Me and thy crying self . . .
> In few, they hurried us aboard a bark,
> Bore us some leagues to sea . . .
>
> (Act I, Scene 2)

Calderón de la Barca, in his masterpiece *La vida es sueño (Life is a*

Dream) describes how his hero, Segismundo, having been brought to the King's palace, becomes infatuated with his cousin Estrella, who is already betrothed to another man, and tries to kiss her hand against her will; a servant interferes, and Segismundo, furious, throws him off the balcony. The servant had been warned by Segismundo, who had told him, in very few words, that he would defenestrate him if need be, but had rejected Segismundo's menace:

> *Con los hombres como yo*
> *no puede hacerse eso.*
>
> (With men like me
> you cannot do such a thing.)

Segismundo then proceeds to throw him down from the high balcony:

> *Cayó del balcon al mar:*
> *¡Vive Dios, que pudo ser!*
>
> (He fell down from the balcony into the sea:
> By my faith, I could do it!)
>
> (Act II, Scene 6)

Yet Calderón could have known (should have known) that the capital of Poland, the city where the King's palace rose, was at that time Krakow, certainly not a seaport. And yet he assumed the King's castle was surrounded by the sea or at least built on the seashore.

Cervantes did not lack for sources of information, however unreliable. We should remember his era was not inclined towards scientific precision. Facts and fantasy often mixed in the travel books he may have read. Perhaps some of the sources that inspired him, if not with respect to concrete details, but rather as a cultural background that explains his cavalier attitude towards geography, were the descriptions of the New World so widely read during his lifetime. Columbus, Hernán Cortés, Bernal Díaz del Castillo, so many other explorers and conquerors, had given the Spaniards an image of the new lands beyond the sea that was at the same time realistic and fantastic. America was different, huge, fabulous. The magnificent exotic cities such as Tenochtitlan were a source of wonder. They seemed to belong in the pages of a novel, a fiction such as *Amadís de Gaula* or the other novels of chivalry. The real world turned out to be more fantastic than the imagination of most writers: it was a mirage come true. Aristotle in his *Poetics* had claimed that art should imitate Nature. Yet in these strange descriptions of the New World one could almost believe that—as Oscar Wilde would claim much later—Nature was imitating art. How could one tell the fantasy apart from the commonplace and factual? Should one even try?

There were numerous books on geography and travel available to Cervantes, and he must have been familiar with some of them: they were easily available in the Spanish libraries and bookstores of his time. Books such as the works of Archbishop Olao Magno of Uppsala, a well-known geographer of the sixteenth century; the *Jardín de flores curiosas (Garden of Curious Flowers)* by Antonio de Torquemada; the *De las cosas maravillosas del mundo (All About the World's Wonders)* by Francisco Thamara; Pero Mexía's *Silva de Varia lección (Gatherings from Many Sources)*, and, of course, classical works such as Marco Polo's description of his travels, the famous works of Pliny, Strabo, and Ptolemy. Many of their tales rivaled in exotic strangeness the marvelous accounts given by Spanish travellers and explorers who came back from the New World or the Pacific Ocean, the "Mar del Sur" or Southern Seas, and often described strange animals, cities of gold, vast cities built in the middle of a lake or on top of a mountain, temples and citadels not unlike the fabled Egyptian pyramids.

And yet it would be wrong to underline excessively Cervantes' disregard of geography; in a way, the opposite is true. Or, rather, the essential facts are true, the details are imagined. All his locations, except one, can be found on the maps of his time, even such seemingly fantastic places as the Island of Fire and the Island of the Hermits. Cervantes does know geography. What happens occasionally is that he is more interested in what we may call "symbolic geography." Let us not forget that the travels of his two lovers take them from the Nordic mists to the clear light of the South. The trip ends in Rome, an exceptional city, the spiritual center of the world. It begins in a strange place, a country not found on any of the maps current in the sixteenth century, in the mythical island of Thule. If we pay attention to this unique lapse, we realize that Cervantes was trying to establish two poles, at the beginning and the end of his book, one remote, mysterious, and on the whole imperfect, negative, the other positive, sacred, luminous. The true allegorical dimensions of Cervantes' novel begin so to appear. As Alban K. Forcione states, in one notable case the importance of symbolic space causes Cervantes to sacrifice geographical precision and verisimilitude. Rome, as *cabeza del mundo* (Head or Center of the world), "Eternal City," and a real city, was well-suited to be the goal of Cervantes' heroes. However, those maps of the time that had the greatest pretensions to scientific accuracy offered no city or country with such symbolic power for the origins of the quest. Hence Cervantes turns to classical geography, locating Periandro's kingdom on Thule. He underscores its traditional associations as a hallowed kingdom and "the end of the earth."[3] The name for this strange land, assumed to be the last land to the West, "the end of the world," can be found in Vergil, in his *Georgics* (Book I), and Cervantes is well aware of it, since he quotes the pertinent passage from Vergil in Chapter 12 of Book IV of *Persiles.* It is curious to observe, at the same time, that Cervantes seems aware of the odd choice he has made as to the point of geographic departure of his characters' adventures, and characteristically he retraces his steps and underplays the symbolism to be found in Thule. Shortly after the allusion to Vergil, a character says: *Tule, que agora vulgarmente se llama Islanda* . . . (Thule, which nowadays people call Iceland . . .), Book IV, Ch. 12. Yet the impression remains: Cervantes is making use here of allegorical space. Could it be that *Persiles* was intended to be much more than a romance, than an endless series of melodramatic adventures, much more than a "Renaissance soap opera"? In order to make perfectly sure that this is the case, it is wise to examine Cervantes' sources: only thus can we ascertain what he imitates and what he innovates, and thus find out what his purpose was.

III *The Sources of Persiles*

The main source for *Persiles* has been identified by most critics as Heliodorus' *Aethiopica,* a Hellenistic romance of the third century A.D. The main reason for this identification is obvious: Cervantes himself points out his indebtedness to Heliodorus when, in his preface to the *Exemplary Novels,* he claims that his work in progress (the *Persiles,* at that time, was still without a title) would try to compete with Heliodorus' novel. It was indeed then a famous novel. Tasso had been influenced by it when in *Gerusalemme Liberata* he created his most interesting feminine character, Clorinda. Its fame would not soon vanish: it was still a "best seller" in France during the seventeenth century. Racine devoured its pages on the sly, as his stern teachers considered the book to be too mundane and frivolous for a good Jansenist mind. It had been translated from the original Greek into French by Jacques Amyot in 1547; the first translation into Spanish, anonymous, was based upon Amyot's version and was published in Antwerp in 1554. The second Spanish version was obtained by comparing a Latin translation and the Greek text. The translator, Fernando de Mena, had it published at Alcalá de Henares in 1587. It is possible that Cervantes owned both Spanish translations, as the *Aethiopica*, otherwise known by its subtitle, *Theagenes and Chariclea*, was one of the favorite books of the Renaissance. The typical characteristics of this novel, as well as of *Apollonius of Tyre* and other romances of the Hellenistic period, are the separation of two lovers, hairbreadth escapes from a series of appalling perils and adversities, a final reunion, and a happy ending.

The *Aethiopica* is a long novel, the longest of all the Hellenistic romances, and perhaps the one to offer its essential traits in the most typical form. Its ten books offer the reader a plot both simple and complex. Let us try to summarize it, since the book is not easy to find for the average reader: its ancient glory has vanished, it is no longer in print in most countries, and on the whole it has not been popular with modern Classical scholars. Chariclea, a beautiful maiden about whose ancestors nothing is known, lives in Delphi, the ancient oracular shrine and precinct of Apollo. She is a priestess at the temple. Theagenes, a Thessalian prince, falls in love with her, suddenly and dramatically, during a party given at the temple, and she reciprocates his love. Protected and accompanied by Calasiris, an Egyptian priest living in Delphi, Theagenes and Chariclea flee together to Egypt, but not before swearing eternal love and chastity until the moment they should marry. The novel is made up of the numerous adventures that befall the lovers before their marriage. There are storms at sea, attacks by pirates and bandits, wars, ambushes, betrayals, mistaken identities, sudden recognitions, live characters confused with dead ones, dead ones that speak, witchcraft, and obstacles of every imaginable kind continually slow up both the action and the happy ending. Finally the lovers arrive in Ethiopia as war prisoners slated to be sacrificed in a barbarous ritual. But in that very moment it is learned that the girl is the daughter of the King of Ethiopia, Idaspe, and Persina, the Queen. And so the last obstacles are overcome and the marriage finally takes place. As in other Greek novels which have been handed down to us, the *Aethiopica* is dominated by the theme of love as a virtuous and proper feeling, crowned by matrimony; it abounds in mannered sentimentality and makes a clear distinction between good and bad characters, with the good ones always winning out at the end, and shows excessive delight in harrowing adventures and in marvelous happenings. Its psychology is rudimentary and conventional, and the characters, seen from the outside, are reduced to caricature-like marionettes. But spectacular descriptions and a kaleidoscope of adventures help to camouflage an inner vacuity. A vague reliogosity, expressed by the cult of Apollo-Helios, is an important ingredient but does not quite succeed in giving unity to the novel.

Finally, the modern reader can easily see through the melodrama, the rhetorical tricks, the conventions: nevertheless, there is something appealing about the basic situation of two young lovers in trouble. The resilience of this novel can be appreciated if we point out that Tasso, Cervantes, countless second-rate novelists in the seventeenth and eighteenth centuries enjoyed it, and moreover, as most lovers of Italian literature may realize—although this fact has been almost completely ignored by serious critics—we can still find echoes of the *Aethiopica's* plot in the best and most popular Italian novel of the nineteenth century, Alessandro Manzoni's *I Promessi Sposi (The Betrothed),* which means that the influence of Heliodorus was to reach, directly or indirectly, into the Romantic era. Few novels can boast about such an enduring presence.

Cervantes wanted to accomplish two goals. The first and foremost aim was, perhaps, to please his readers, to compose a novel which would be successful. This goal was easily attained: *Persiles* enjoyed an immediate success comparable to that of *Don Quixote.* The years that followed its posthumous publication in 1617 witnessed ten editions in Spanish, translations into French, Italian, and English, and imitations in drama and prose fiction. This success was not of short duration: in the eighteenth century, new editions, translations, and imitations continued to appear. At the beginning of the

nineteenth century, a serious scholar, the Swiss Jean-Charles
Simonde de Sismondi, could claim, in his *De la littérature du midi
de l'Europe*, published in 1813, that many readers considered it to
be Cervantes' masterpiece. Obviously, the best way to produce a
modern best seller, Cervantes concluded, was to imitate an old best
seller. Cervantes turned to a model that was universally praised for
its sound structure, its moving situations, its use of suspense.

Yet winning the applause of the crowds was not enough for Cervantes. He wanted to please the most demanding critics. They were
all, or almost all, imbued with the ideas about literature that Aristotle had propounded in his *Poetics*. One of the rules suggested for
the epic poems, the highest form of literature, was to begin in the
middle of a significant episode, in order to involve the reader in the
action. It is curious to observe that Heliodorus makes use of this
technique, and that Cervantes follows suit, thereby bringing his
romance one step closer to what we might call an "epic narrative,"
a prose epic. In the case of Heliodorus, his French translator,
Jacques Amyot, had already remarked, in the preface to his version,
upon this strange technique: ". . . it is strangely organized, for he
begins in the middle of his tale, as Heroic Poets often do. Which at
first creates a great surprise among his readers, and awakens in
them a passionate desire to hear the beginning of the story; and yet
he compels them to go on reading through the ingenious linking of
his plot, so that one is not quite certain about what happens at the
beginning of the first book until one reads the end of the fifth book.
And when the reader reaches this point, he is still more anxious to
find out about the end than he was when he started his reading of
the novel. In this fashion his critical judgement remains always in
suspense, until he reaches the conclusion, which satisfies him fully,
as are satisfied those who finally enjoy the fact that they have at last
reached a goal long desired."[4]

These remarks by the French translator of Heliodorus raise an interesting problem. Both *Aethiopica* and *Persiles* are links in a chain
which stretches from Classical literature to the present, and which
establishes the novel as an accepted literary genre. Modern readers
do not realize how difficult it was for the novel to be born and be
accepted: It was the "ugly duckling," the disinherited genre.
Aristotle does not even mention it in his *Poetics*, a basic book which
sets the tone for literary critics from the fourth century B.C. up to

the Romantic era. Was it perhaps a careless omission on his part? It does not seem possible. The Greeks did not assign a Muse to the art of the novel. They had a Muse presiding over the creation of historians, one for choreographers, one for astronomers, no muse for aspiring novelists. Critics acquainted with Chinese literature report the same strange phenomenon: the novel is in Chinese letters, until very recent times, a despised genre, one utterly lacking in prestige, to be left to rank amateurs and pornographers.

It is possible that novelists such as Heliodorus, trying to establish their craft in spite of the lack of official academic recognition, may have borrowed some of the techniques prescribed by Aristotle and his followers for epic poets and dramatists, such as the *in-medias-res* beginning and the need for unity of the work and verisimilitude in its plot.

Heliodorus, about whom very little is known, must have felt in his creative years the pull of two opposite forces. On the one hand, he wanted to please his readers; on the other, he did not want to antagonize the masters of rhetoric and Aristotelian critics who exerted a strong influence upon the most cultivated and influential public of that era. Similarly, perhaps yet with greater urgency, Cervantes felt the need to placate both groups. This tension was not uncommon during the Renaissance. Both Lope de Vega and Shakespeare were keenly aware of these two goals.

IV *Aristotle's Influence*

It seems evident that both Heliodorus and Aristotle were essential in the birth of *Persiles:* both were its sources, if we understand the word "sources" in a wide sense, not only the materials that an author can use in his work but also the techniques that can give shape to his materials. Cervantes was highly sensitive to the critical currents of his age. His *Don Quixote* is, as some of his modern critics as Edward C. Riley are aware, both a novel and a tract of literary criticism. How could Cervantes fail to take into account, while writing *Persiles*, the very principles of criticism that he had propounded in *Don Quixote?*

The answer is simple: he did take them into account. *Persiles*, no less than *Don Quixote*, although in a less obvious fashion, is a critique and a purification of the "wrong" type of novel, the romances of chivalry. As Alban Forcione states, "if it could ever be said that a work of literature is almost exclusively a product of literature and literary theory, it could be said of Cervantes' final work *Los Trabajos de Persiles y Sigismunda*. Everywhere the eclectic character of the work is visible: in its undisguised appropriation of scenes and passages from Vergil's *Aeneid* and Heliodorus' *Ethiopian History*, in its inclusion of an Italian novella and many brief reminiscences from biblical tradition, medieval romance, and other works of classical antiquity, and in its presentation of various recurrent topics of imaginative literature which are as old as literature itself. Moreover, the specific literary theories which inspired the fusion of so many widely disparate elements into a coherent whole are everywhere apparent in its texture. They are revealed in occasional digressions about aesthetic problems and in brief remarks of the self-conscious narrator drawing attention to the criteria governing his selective processes in the inclusion of a specific element. But more basically they become deeply imbedded in the action of the work itself informing an extended dramatic situation and its development in the second book."[5]

The discovery and diffusion of Aristotle's *Poetics*, on the one hand, and the aesthetic critique of the romances of chivalry, on the other, had created for Cervantes the need to establish new rules for his fiction. Foreign critics were unsparing in their judgment of contemporary Spanish fiction. Cervantes was probably aware of the harsh words used by the Italian critic Giovanni Battista Pigna, who in his treatise *I romanzi*, published in 1554, states that "nearly all the Spanish romances are full of worthless follies, being founded, as they are, solely on miraculous occurrences and with their supernatural spirits of one sort or another always bringing about things far removed from the natural world and from true pleasure, which is generally produced by legitimate marvels . . . [The Spanish romances] have the custom of presenting journeys by horse without taking into account the sea which lies between the rider and destination, and they present journeys by ship although there is land there to oppose such passage; they make the short roads long and the long ones short, and they include places which are not in the world; moreover, they lose themselves continually in love affairs and empty reasonings. There are nearly always in the battles described by the Spanish romances the most impossible things accepted as the most true."[6]

Around the middle of the sixteenth century, literary critics started to make systematic use of Aristotle's *Poetics* for their attacks on the romances of chivalry. Their objections to this literary genre were manifold: lack of verisimilitude, lack of artistic unity, lack of sound moral teachings. In Spain the attack of intelligent critics such as Luis Vives was based mainly upon moral grounds, but also on traditional arguments derived from Plato: these books were a waste of time, a distraction from serious scientific work. Literature of this kind, Plato had claimed, is fictitious, it consists of lies. Vives denies that there can be any pleasure for the reader "in things that they (the authors of romances of chivalry) feign so foolishly and openly," as, for instance, when they describe a battle in which one knight kills thirty opponents and two giants, and recovers with miraculous swiftness from the wounds he sustained in battle. Vives concludes, "Is it not madness to be carried away by such idiocies and to be impressed by them?"[7]

As Alban Forcione ably states, "it is only against this background of literary theorizing that we can properly understand Cervantes' undeniably high literary aspirations in the conception of the *Persiles*, his desire to rival Heliodorus, his theorizing concerning the purification of the romance of chivalry and the creation of an epic in prose, the important thematic role that contemporary literary theory—particularly those problems surrounding the polemics over Ariosto and Tasso—has in both the *Quixote* and the *Persiles*, the creation of the *Persiles*, and finally the literary humor which functions so successfully in the context of the *Quixote* but gives the *Persiles* a puzzling ambivalence."[8] Cervantes had dealt with literary theory in *Don Quixote*, especially in the chapters where the knight's literary taste is discussed by the Curate, at the beginning of the novel (Part I, Chapter 6, in which the scrutiny of the knight's library takes place) and in Chapters 49 and 50 of the same part where Don Quixote and the Canon of Toledo argue at length about the truth and literary merit of the romances of chivalry.

The Canon of Toledo had undoubtedly read with care Aristotle's *Poetics.* Judged by Aristotle's formula that an epic poem should have for its subject "a single action, whole and complete, with a beginning, a middle, and an end,"[9] the romances of chivalry, which in the sixteenth century were often classified as epic poems, turned out to be at best many actions of one man, at worst many actions of many; their composition was faulty, even chaotic. One of the Canon's criticisms of these novels centers on their structural disorder. The

Canon, who, as we have said, had read Aristotle, seems to have been equally acquainted with Horace's aesthetic ideas, as expounded in the *Epistle to the Pisos*, or, as it is more generally known, *Ars Poetica*. Horace begs the poets to avoid creating a composition that recalls to the reader's mind the chaotic appearance of a monster. Aristotle wants the work of literature to resemble a unified, living organism which must be entirely visible to the glance of the beholder. The Canon makes use of an analogy which was used by many theorists of the century who criticized the multiplicity of plot and protagonist in the romances of chivalry: "I have never seen a book of chivalry with a whole body for a plot, with all its limbs complete, so that the middle corresponds to the beginning, and the end to the beginning and middle, for they are generally made up of so many limbs that they seem intended rather to form a chimera or a monster then a well-proportioned figure."[10] He proceeds to invoke the principle of verisimilitude, another important line of attack of the critics of that period when dealing with fantastic fiction: "What beauty can there be, or what harmony between the parts and the whole, or between the whole and its parts, in a book or story in which a sixteen-year-old lad deals a giant as tall as a tower one blow with his sword . . .?"[11] Chapter 47 of *Don Quixote* (Part I) is also relevant to this aesthetic debate: in it the Canon declares that ". . . in works of fiction there should be a mating between the plot and the readers' intelligence. They should be so written that the impossible is made to appear possible, things hard to believe being smoothed over and the mind held in suspense in such a manner as to create surprise and astonishment while at the same time they divert and entertain so that admiration and pleasure go hand in hand. But these are things which he cannot accomplish who flees verisimilitude and the imitation of nature, qualities that go to constitute perfection in the art of writing."[12]

And yet Cervantes is not wholly convinced by the arguments of the Aristotelian critics. His mental reservations come to the surface time and time again. He must have thought them, on the whole, pedantic. Moreover, they were not acquainted with the problems of a professional writer of fiction. The words ". . . and the mind held in suspense," in the above quotation, are revealing. Only through suspense (which presupposes an identification, partial or complete, between reader and hero) can the reader enjoy a long novel. His reservations about the harsh judgment meted out to the romances of chivalry may have prompted him to state (ironically, he places these words in the mouth of the Canon, who had been so merciless in his criticism): ". . . for all the harsh things that he had said of such books, the Canon added, he had found one good thing about them, and that was the chance they afforded for a good mind to display its true worth, for they offered a broad and spacious field over which the author's pen might run without impediment, describing shipwrecks, tempests, battles, and encounters . . . he could picture here a lovely lady, modest, discreet, and reserved, and there a Christian knight, gentle and brave, setting a lawless, barbarous braggart over against a prince, courtly, valorous and benign, letting us see at once the loyalty and devotion of the vassals and the generosity of their lords."[13] Chapter 47 concludes on a positive note: these books, the Canon claims, "indeed, by their very nature, provide the author with an unlimited field in which to try his hand at the epic, lyric, tragic, and comic genres and depict in turn all the moods that are represented by these most sweet and pleasing branches of poetry and oratory; for the epic may be written in prose as well as in verse."[14]

Here we have, in a nutshell, the plan that Cervantes was to follow in his *Persiles.* He would write a romance that would please the crowds but at the same time be as similar as possible to a prose epic. It would be a novel that, according to the Canon's words, "keeping the mind in suspense, may so astonish, hold, excite, and entertain, that wonder and pleasure go hand in hand." He would avoid, as far as possible, the presentation of realities that did not exist in the natural world, e.g., giants as big as towers, imaginary geographical settings, such as the lands of Prester John of the Indies, and countries that Ptolemy never knew nor Marco Polo visited.

As Alban Forcione sees it, "it is clear that the Canon of Toledo's plan for the ideal book of chivalry was Cervantes' general formula for the *Persiles,* and it is tempting to believe that the hundred pages which the Canon claims to have written and abandoned are Cervantes' first sketch of his final work. Just how far the composition of the *Persiles* can be related to the suggestive literary dialogue is conjectural. Nevertheless, Cervantes' desire to follow the classical rules—unity, verisimilitude, decorum, the legitimized marvelous, rhetorical display, moral edification, and instructive erudition—is everywhere evident in the *Persiles*, both in subject matter and structure and in the various comments of the self-conscious narrator concerning criteria governing his creative and selective process."[15]

What Cervantes knew instinctively, and his contemporary Aristotelian critics forgot, was that a long narrative in prose had to be built around certain poles of tension, around emotional cores. Tension could not be sustained indefinitely: pauses were also essential. The romances of chivalry were organized along such lines. But in these romances tension was provided by the frantic moments of activity of the hero or heroes, the struggles, the scenes of battle, which, in turn, meant that for this tension to be relieved many implausible factors had to be introduced. Tension was created by pitting a hero against impossible odds: it was brought down to a lower level by having the hero óvercome every obstacle, which in turn compelled the writer to resort to magic and the supernatural. These romances are, in modern terms, much closer to the adventures of Superman than to the modern thrillers of espionage built around our contemporary hero, James Bond. Cervantes would follow Heliodorus, a sounder model than the authors of the romances of chivalry; tension would be created in his *Persiles*, suspense and empathy achieved, through psychological devices, especially through the constant dangers menacing the happiness of the young couple and the painful separations forced on them by their enemies, by accidents, storms, and sheer bad luck. Where the writers of romances of chivalry tried mainly to create admiration in their readers by describing the extravagant and superhuman adventures of one or several heroes, Cervantes wants to elicit from his readers feelings of compassion, sympathy, concern.

And yet Cervantes' novel differs from Heliodorus' *Aethiopica* in many respects. This fact had already been noticed in 1854 by the English translator of the *Persiles*, who signs his Preface with the initials "L. D. S." and has been identified as Louisa Dorothea Stanley: she points out that "though the *plan* of *Persiles and Sigismunda* is taken from Heliodorus, I do not think they have *any* resemblance in style, and there is far more vivacity and humour in the narrative and characters (in Cervantes' novel), and more nature too, in spite of the high flown romance that surrounds them." She goes on to warn the reader: "I fear the modern reader will find the numerous episodes tedious; and story after story, which every additional personage we meet, thinks it necessary to relate, will perhaps try his patience; yet there is great beauty in many of these, at least in the original language."[16] Her statement is plausible. The Spanish text does sound more harmonious, does have a more supple rhythm than its English versions. Modern readers do find many of the pages somewhat tedious. This is perhaps due to two factors. The first is easily explained: Cervantes' main literary device, or perhaps main stylistic device, is suspense. But our readers are used to a faster pace and a stronger dose of suspense. Cervantes' suspense is subtle and slow in developing, as the main narrative, the one that can create suspense inasmuch as the fate of the two young lovers depends on what happens in this main tale, is constantly interrupted by new characters and new tales related to these characters. Cervantes' contemporaries had apparently an inexhaustible supply of patience and were perhaps inclined towards masochism.

The second factor which prevents us from enjoying *Persiles* to the full is that Cervantes is operating, throughout the novel, at several levels. The superficial level, the one that the reader understands right away, is made up of the adventures of the two star-crossed lovers. The deeper meaning has been pointed out by modern critics: Thus Alban Forcione states that the *Persiles* is a quest romance in which the heroes must abandon an imperfect society, journey through strange worlds full of menacing forces, and suffer numerous trials and struggles before reaching their destination.[17] Here their sufferings are rewarded with superior wisdom, and they can return to elevate their society to the state of perfection which they themselves embody. This process of purification, of groping from darkness and shadow towards light, of attaining wisdom through suffering and through faithful, chaste love, is not unlike the process prescribed by Plato in his *Republic,* in which men are described inside a cave, surrounded by shadows; the light shines outside the cave, but only philosophers will be able to venture outside the cave, after which they should return to the cave in order to enlighten their fellowmen and bring to them the fruits of wisdom.

At another level the quest of the young lovers reenacts the basic myth of Christianity: Man in his fallen state must wander in the sublunary world of disorder, suffering in the world of human history, and be reborn through expiation and Christ's mercy. Here again we move from darkness towards light, from a realm menaced by war, an oppressive king, and the threat of sterility to the city of Rome, which traditionally brings to our mind the Kingdom of the Blessed.

Possibly the taste of most modern readers does not favor extended allegory in a novel. In any case, few readers of Cervantes' novel are aware, nowadays, of the mythical and allegorical dimensions of the book. It can be doubted that many readers of Cervantes' own time were aware of it, in spite of the fact that allegory was far from dead during the Renaissance.

In this respect, the *Persiles* is entirely different from its model, *Aethiopica;* Cervantes' pride, his ambition as a writer, prevented him from following too closely a model and forced him to endow his novel with a complicated symbolical scaffolding that some readers would be capable of understanding and appreciating. He places a few clues here and there, strategically, all along his work, clues which indicate to the alert reader that Cervantes is not content with producing a mere romance. For instance, in the very first pages we find the theme of bondage, the theme of darkness, the quest for freedom. The *in-medias-res* beginning adds to the tension and suspense. Chapter 1 bears the following title: "Periander is drawn up out of the Dungeon: he goes out to Sea on a Raft: a Tempest comes on, and he is saved by a Ship." What follows is a scene worthy of a Gothic novel, a scene, moreover, that would bring to mind to Cervantes' readers the scenes of Calderón's *La vida es sueño* if it had been published or staged at that time (as is well known, Calderón's play follows Cervantes' novel, not vice versa).

Darkness and danger are everywhere in these first lines: "Near the mouth of a deep and narrow dungeon, which was more like a tomb than a prison to its wretched inmates, stood Corsicurbo, the barbarian. He shouted with a terrible voice, but, although the fearful clamour was heard far and near, none could hear his words distinctly, except the miserable Clelia, an unhappy captive, buried in this abyss. 'Clelia,' he said, 'see that the boy who was committed to your custody two days ago, be bound fast to the cord I am about to let down; see that his hands are tied behind him, and make him ready to be drawn up here: also look well if among the women of the last prize there are any beautiful enough to deserve being brought amongst us, and to enjoy the light of the clear sky that is above us.' So saying, he let down a strong hempen cord, and for some brief space he and four other barbarians pulled it, until, with his hands tied strongly behind him, they drew up a boy, seemingly about nineteen or twenty years of age, drest in linen like a mariner, but beautiful, exceedingly."[18]

A novel, unlike an opera, does not usually start with an overture. Yet the first chapter of the *Persiles* has the same function as an opera overture: it introduces the main themes, the theme of ascension from darkness to light and the theme of geographical flight towards freedom. Vertical movement and horizontal travel are related, the symbolic ascent and the painful horizontal movement towards freedom, light, wisdom.

Periandro, the young man in the first chapter, is, of course, Persiles, the lover of Sigismunda; their travels, both real and symbolic, become the unifying thread in this long and complex novel. Travels, tribulations, dangers: the pages of Cervantes' novel remind us of *Pilgrim's Progress* and of the serial film, *The Perils of Pauline.* Symbols and pathos abound: we long for comic relief. We discover the importance of the motif of *los trabajos* ("the works") in the Spanish title of the novel, which becomes a principle of unity. The Spanish dictionaries of the Renaissance, specifically the dictionary compiled by Covarrubias, offer two meanings of the word *trabajos.* It means "work" or "task," and also "ordeal" or "trial." This second meaning is especially relevant. The novel narrates an ordeal, a trial, in which two young people will be able to prove their lasting love and also their patience, perseverance, and faith in God in adversity.

Light and darkness alternate along the pages of Cervantes' novel. The events unfold according to a pattern that avoids the impossible, miraculous effects dear to the writers of romances of chivalry and justly criticized by the Aristotelian critics. Cervantes tries to respect verisimilitude. But he wants to organize the many strands that are woven into his complex tapestry in as clear a pattern as possible. No scene repeats exactly a previous scene, yet we have often an impression of *déjà-vu.* This is perhaps due to the fact that all his characters are searchers: they want to find peace and wisdom, they want to emerge from the shadows into the light, they are moreover, in their search, looking for a central point in which they will find peace and wisdom. Many contemporary anthropologists and specialists of comparative religions would conclude that Cervantes' characters are not, in this respect, unique, bizarre, atypical. On the contrary, these characters retrace their steps, undergo similar adventures, repeat their efforts, simply because they are looking for the same goal: the center of the world.

Yet their search takes them through a labyrinth. It is a path with blind alleys, strange encounters. Oriental cultures have evolved a unique graphic design in which a labyrinth, often a circle surrounded by a square and divided into connecting sections, stands for the universe: men can accept it as a map, one to be followed in their wanderings, in search of the goal, the center, where circle, square, and labyrinth will finally disappear when the wanderer attains his goal, union with the cosmos. The composition of the *Persiles* resembles in many ways this Oriental design, this *mandala*, and this labyrinth. In it we find also blind alleys, connecting roads, strange encounters.

The connecting stories, the unfolding tales, the recurrent patterns of Cervantes' novel compel us to conjecture that Heliodorus and Aristotle were not his only guides, his basic sources. Oriental literature abounds in complex works where the unfolding of the plot brings us to numerous crossroads, to blind alleys, to "the tale-within-the-tale." The most outstanding example of such labyrinthine composition is, of course, *The Thousand and One Nights*, the complicated juxtaposition and interpolation of stories that have delighted countless generations of Oriental and Western readers. It is not necessary to prove—an impossible task—that Cervantes was acquainted with this Arabic-Persian-Oriental compilation. We might point out that he was one of the very few European writers of his century to have lived for a while in a Moslem environment, yet this would not be a conclusive proof. Let us state simply that the *Persiles*, just like *The Thousand and One Nights*, reminds us of a labyrinth.

And yet it differs from the Oriental collection of tales in one significant respect: the beginning and the end of the labyrinth are clearly marked in Cervantes' novel, in a way that gives it true symbolic meaning. To be sure, both the complex book built around the story of Scheherazade and the complicated story woven by Heliodorus around his two young lovers have clear beginnings and ends. Yet they lack symbolic content. Heliodorus, it is said, was Bishop of Tricca, in Thessaly, and wrote in a time when the rise of Christianity should have made both him and his readers sensitive to religious meanings. It is Cervantes, a lay writer, who is closer to real religious writing: his fable compels us often to gaze upwards, to the heavenly places from which Fate, or Providence, pulls the strings; and it is organized in a seesaw movement between the sad moments of "purgatory," i.e., the times when the lovers are imprisoned or isolated from each other, and the ecstatic visions of bliss. The vision of Rome from the top of a hill is one of these moments: the young lovers proceed to renew their vows and rekindle their hope; their heavenly vision does not exclude earthly love; as Persiles says to his beloved Sigismunda, "Already is the air of Rome playing on our cheeks, and the hopes that have supported us are beating in our hearts; already it seems to me that I am in possession of the beloved object so long desired. Look well, O Lady, whether your feelings still remain unchanged; scrutinize well your heart, and see if it is still firm and true to its first intentions, or will be after you have fulfilled your vow, which I doubt not that it will, for your royal blood cannot deceive nor give false promises. Let me then hear you say, O lovely Sigismunda, that the Periander you see before you, is the Persiles that you saw in the palace of my royal father; the same Persiles who pledged his word to you to be your husband there, and who would gladly fulfill that promise in the Deserts of Lybia, should our adverse fortune take us there . . . Why should we not be the fabricators of our own fortune? They say every man makes his own from beginning to end. I will not answer for what I may do after our happy fate has united us; the inconvenience of our present divided state will soon be over, when we are one; there are fields enough where we can maintain ourselves, cottages wherein we may find shelter and clothes to cover us; for as to the happiness two souls made one can feel, it is as you say unequalled by any other, and we could not enjoy *this* beneath the gilded roofs of a palace."[19] Love creates its own sacred places. Man—and woman—take at last a firm hold on their destiny. We know at this moment that the novel is going to have a happy ending.

V   *The Final Message*

A Spanish critic, Agustín González de Amezúa, has pointed out the aspects of Heliodorus' novel that made it so attractive to Cervantes and to the Spaniards of the Golden Age: "Heliodorus' novel marks the acceptance and glorification of two human values triumphant above others in Spain's Golden Age. On the one hand, a love for adventure, for the unknown, the marvelous; on the other, a latent idealism, an aspiration towards an idyllic world, with the worship of the noblest virtues and feelings of man: faithfulness in love, purity, a spirit of abnegation and sacrifice, faithfulness to one's own ideas, all of which make the protagonists of Heliodorus' *Aethiopica* into admirable prototypes of human virtue. All these values, I repeat, were dearly beloved by the Spaniards of that period, whether simple novelists or men of erudition, and in finding them sublimated in a novel which contained as well a fine composition and rare literary beauty, they saw in Heliodorus a great novelist, one admired and emulated by all."[20]

Yet Cervantes' novel was far better than its model. It meant, for him as well as for his readers, an escape to a world of marvelous adventures, a world of dangers and of freedom, of destiny and of love. There is a link between Cervantes' last novel and the romances of chivalry that he had criticized in *Don Quixote:* both in the romances and in the *Persiles* the heroic effort of the main characters is victorious at the end. The *Persiles* is more realistic than *Aethiopica,* and of course much more in tune with history, geography, and common sense, than the romances of chivalry. It is also a work of art: its style is extremely pleasant to the Spanish eye and the Spanish ear (many passages, read aloud in the original, have musical overtones: harmony, rhythm, well-rounded sentences, amplifications and variations on a main theme; it is possible to speak of "leit-motifs," just as in Wagner's music, through which Cervantes presents throughout his book the theme of purgatory, i.e., the separation and anguish of the two unhappy lovers, and paradise, i.e., the hope of reunion and fulfillment).

It is no wonder, then, that this novel attained an immediate success comparable to that of *Don Quixote.* Cervantes seems to have had a premonition of this success: the fact that he was working on a novel that was sure to become a "best seller" may have sustained his strength and given him a new lease on life. He had to finish his manuscript at all costs.

Ten editions were published in the years immediately following its posthumous publication in 1617, as well as translations into French, Italian, and English, and imitations in prose fiction and in drama. New imitations and editions appeared in the eighteenth century. At the beginning of the nineteenth century, the Swiss scholar

Sismondi could still claim that many readers considered it to be Cervantes' masterpiece.[21]

Many modern critics, as well as many modern readers, have been less kind to Cervantes' last novel. Thus Mack Singleton, for instance, claims (against the opinion of practically every other Hispanist who has dealt with the subject) that the *Persiles* was for Cervantes merely a "pot boiler," a clumsy adventure story written by Cervantes in his youth and wisely kept well hidden by its author until money was short and death was fast approaching.[22]

Yet contemporary criticism is becoming increasingly interested in Cervantes' last novel. It is seen by some as a neglected masterpiece. As one of these critics states, "it is only in the last twenty-five years that criticism has begun to take the *Persiles* seriously, to see it in its historical circumstances rather than in the context of contemporary literary preferences, and to consider it as an independent work of art. The exploration of the great impact of Neoclassical literary theory on Cervantes, as well as the study of Renaissance discussions and evaluations of Heliodorus' *Aethiopica,* has thrown much light on Cervantes' intentions and aspirations in his final work. We may still agree with Menéndez y Pelayo that Cervantes' decision to imitate the Greek romance was a lamentable piece of folly, but we may at least admit that Renaissance critical opinion considered the work to be an artfully constructed epic in prose and a model for all who dared to scale the heights of Parnassus."[23]

More than its episodic panorama and its proliferating action, what interests the modern critics in this novel is its structure, its pattern: a coherent cycle of catastrophe and restoration linked symbolically to the Christian vision of man's fall and redemption. Cervantes wanted to create an epic in prose. What he did in fact write was an allegorical romance in which recurrent motifs and myths manage to unify the action by endowing it with a ritualistic quality.

Every light projects a shadow. Every positive aspect in this novel can be seen as the opposite of a mistake or a defect—at least to the modern reader. The characters of *Persiles* move ecstatically, like stars in orbit. This is a source of strength in one sense, but also a weakness. For these characters were created perfect: they do not evolve. Their creator placed them on a Platonic pedestal at the very beginning of the tale, and there they remain, surrounded by a magic halo, eternal, changeless. The reader misses the complex and exciting process that makes Don Quixote occasionally sensitive to the common sense of Sancho Panza, that makes Sancho respond to the lofty goals of his master and thus become slowly "quixote-like" or "quixotized." Our own experience, and the writings of modern psychologists, have made us aware of the changing nature of man, of man's recurrent crises of identity, of human interaction. It is not that man's obsessions (if love can be called an obsession) can no longer be the subject of modern novels. It is rather that we are as much aware of man's changeable nature as we are of man's faithfulness or his obsessive nature. This modern awareness makes the *Persiles*, with its perfect, changeless lovers, difficult to accept. We long for the "flesh and blood" characters that Cervantes creates in his best novellas and also in *Don Quixote*. The young lovers in the *Persiles* are models of human behavior: can we identify with such lofty paradigms? Cervantes' last novel is also atypical in one respect: there is very little humor in its adventures. The familiar landmarks, which we may accept as symbolic, are there: the city and the open road. The city is a place of rest and fulfillment, the open road stands for the trials and perils that await those that would reach the city.

Jung has written that ". . . wandering is a symbol of longing, of the restless urge which never finds its object, of nostalgia for the lost mother" and also "The city is a maternal symbol, a woman who harbours the inhabitants in herself like children." [24] As the characters in his novel were about to reach their goal, Cervantes was preparing to make his own serene departure from the world of unfulfilled desire that he had known all through his life, hoping to find repose at the bottom of Being. In his prologue to the *Persiles* (and it is a well-known fact that a prologue to a novel is always written after the novel has been completed), Cervantes makes his final adieu to his friends and readers. He envisions himself as following the path that took his lovers into serene happiness. He takes leave of the world, symbolized in the picturesque figure of a student who overtakes him on the road, pays homage to him as the "delight of the Muses," and leaves him at the gate of Toledo to follow his own way. Cervantes embraces the student: it is an embrace of reconciliation between the man and the adversities that had troubled him for so long. He does not go away with an embittered heart. On the contrary, he keeps hoping that he will some day, somehow, be able to work again, to influence once more his readers: "Here we reached the bridge of

Toledo, over which my road lay, and he separated from me to go by that of Segovia. As to what will be said of my adventure, Fame will take care of that, my friends will have pleasure telling it, and I greater pleasure in hearing it. He again embraced me, I returned the compliment. He spurred on his ass, and left me as sorrily disposed as he was sorrily mounted. He had however furnished me with abundant materials for pleasant writing, but all times are not alike. Perhaps a time may come when, talking up this broken thread again, I may add what is now wanting and what I am aware is needed. Adieu to gaiety, adieu to wit, adieu, my pleasant friends, for I am dying, yet hoping to see you all again happy in another world."[25] These are probably the last words he wrote, just as the *Persiles* is his swan song.

CHAPTER 9

Cervantes Across the Centuries: A Summation

I An Enduring Success

C ERVANTES'S influence has always been linked to the reception accorded to his masterpiece, *Don Quixote*. It is probable that, had he not written his great novel, his position in Spanish letters would still be considerable. Some of his *Exemplary Novels*, expecially *Rinconete and Cortadillo, The Deceitful Marriage, The Dogs' Colloquy,* and *The Glass Scholar,* would have insured him an honorable place among prose writers of the Golden Age. Some of his *Interludes* were bound to become a model for future Spanish writers of comic plays. His international prestige, however, begins and ends with *Don Quixote.* With this novel he became, from the seventeenth century to our own time, a decisive influence in the development of fiction. In Spanish literature, as seen not only by his own countrymen, but by the rest of the world, he became *primus inter pares,* the first and foremost writer in his own literature, a writer to be compared with Shakespeare, Goethe, Molière, Dante, or Dostoevski: one of the unquestioned greats of world literature.

At the very end of his novel, Cervantes wanted to establish clearly, with the help of witnesses, and giving clear details about the fact, Don Quixote's death: "perceiving that their friend was no more, the Curate asked the notary to be a witness to the fact that Alonso Quijano the Good, commonly known as Don Quixote, was truly dead, this being necessary in order that some author other than Cid Hamete Benengeli might not have the opportunity of falsely resurrecting him and writing endless histories of his exploits" (II, 73).[1] Cervantes missed his goal. Don Quixote is, in his spiritual and moral influence, still very much alive. Paradoxically, some modern critics, such as the great Spanish philosopher and essayist Miguel de Unamuno, seem to think that Don Quixote is much more "real," relevant, influential, than his creator, Cervantes. For Unamuno, the son—Don Quixote—has obscured the father's existence, made him dispensable: Cervantes was perhaps not quite aware of the meaning and importance of his hero. Incidentally, I would hesitate to recommend this interpretation to any serious student of the Spanish Golden Age: Unamuno's interpretation, *Vida de Don Quijote y Sancho (The Life of Don Quixote and Sancho.)* The book is perhaps more useful to those readers interested in the heroic and complex personality of Unamuno than to the true *aficionados* of Cervantes and Don Quixote.

It is perhaps unnecessary to repeat here what every lover of Spanish literature knows: *Don Quixote* is not a "literary miracle," a novel born by chance in a desert: it springs from a rich tradition, from a soil that gave birth, among other masterpieces too numerous to list, to the *Cid* epic poem, the ribald yet wise pages of the Archpriest of Hita, the passionate—and cynical—dialogues of Fernando de Rojas' *La Celestina*, a literature, moreover, that would take to heart Cervantes' lessons and translate them to a more contemporary language in the great novels of Benito Pérez Galdós, such as *Misericordia (Compassion)* and *Fortunata y Jacinta (A Tale of Two Women: Fortunata and Jacinta)*, not to mention some of the best pages written in our century by Unamuno and Ortega y Gasset. Cervantes' great novel is therefore, for the whole spectrum of Spanish culture, a summation and a synthesis. It takes into account the epic spirit of the Medieval past as well as the critical mind of the Renaissance and the picaresque cynical attitudes. It is this that makes possible its enduring success both in Spain and in the whole Western world. *Don Quixote* has from age to age revealed a rich panorama of meanings in the wake of extremely diverse critical interpretations. Every period has plucked from it those traits that most markedly came within its own way of understanding and defining the human psyche and its own artistic creations.

The world's readers have never become cold or indifferent to Cervantes' creation: despite constant changes in taste, it would be difficult to discover a period in which *Don Quixote* ceased to be read and praised. On the contrary, as the years went on the main

characters of Cervantes' novel acquired an archetypal nature and
lent themselves to inexhaustible commentaries—to the point that
the bibliography dealing with Cervantes' masterpiece has become so
massive that it is fair to state that no specialist in Cervantes' life and
works is capable of reading even half of the printed materials dealing
with his subject.

The success of Cervantes' great novel first became obvious during
the author's life, when sixteen editions of his novel were printed
within the short span between the first edition and Cervantes' death.
It was, according to all the rules of the period, and also of our own
times, a "best seller," and although each edition added nothing to
Cervantes' pocketbook, it did increase his literary prestige. Man
does not live by bread alone, and Cervantes was not greedy for
money, only for enduring fame (in this respect, as in every other, he
was an eminently wise man). Thanks to numerous translations, Cervantes' fame soon spread beyond the borders of his country. *Don
Quixote* was considered the most amusing book of the century.

Spain was very much in the news all over Europe; Spanish
literature was popular in most of Western Europe. *Don Quixote* was,
moreover, a book in which a Spaniard poked fun at certain
weaknesses (excessive pride, arrogance, blind idealism, lack of common sense, lack of critical spirit) that many Europeans, who for
political and sometimes religious reasons had become anti-Spanish,
thought to be defects peculiar to Spain. *Don Quixote* was thus
doubly welcome, as a great comic masterpiece and a criticism of
Spanish excesses. This attitude is especially clear in France, where
an anti-Spanish attitude had taken shape as a result, partly, of the
numerous wars with Spain, especially the wars that took place
between the French King, Francis I, and the Spanish King and
Emperor, Charles V. Was *Don Quixote* a parody of the heroic ideals
of the Holy Roman Empire? Could the Spanish knight's defeat, at
the end of Part II, presage the end of the myth of Spanish invin-
cibility? We know that, strictly speaking, a literary work should be
judged on its merits as a work of art. Yet the public often buys and
reads books for reasons that have little to do with literature. *Don
Quixote* was read and loved as an amusing book and also, outside
Spain, out of curiosity for everything Spanish or out of a desire to see
Spanish idealism humiliated through parody and farce. But Cervantes' novel was not taken seriously by the critics of his time, who

on the whole paid scant attention to contemporary fiction. The novel was still a new genre, closer to a pastime than to real art. Aristotle had excluded it, or so it seemed, from his list of literary genres. Cervantes' novel was therefore either ignored or dismissed with contempt by many Spanish men of letters. "There is no one so stupid as to praise *Don Quixote*," Lope de Vega had stated.[2] Quevedo and Gracián concurred. Cervantes' style, moreover, was too simple and direct for the new Baroque taste—yet it translated better than Quevedo's nervous, contorted prose.

Within seven years after the publication of Part II in 1615, the book had been translated into French, German, Italian, and English. The first English version was Thomas Shelton's version of Part I, published in London in 1612, Part II appearing in 1620. Hastily written (the First Part was completed in forty days) and too literal, it has, however, the advantage of preserving the flavor of the English of Shakespeare's times. In Italy Cervantes' novel was often read in the original (many Italians of the seventeenth century spoke and read Spanish) and in the translation by Lorenzo Franciosini of 1622.

Until the great and enduring success of Cervantes in eighteenth-century England and nineteenth-century Germany, one could have imagined *Don Quixote* would suffer the fate of most best sellers: instant fame followed by instant oblivion. Yet Cervantes' novel refused to die. The English readers were the first to feel the need for scholarly and detailed commentaries on the text. Edmond Gayton produced an annotated edition in 1654; it was followed by the critical commentaries of Stevens (1700), Ozelle (1725), Jarvis (1742), and John Bowle (1781, much better than the others.) Cervantes was still a prophet without honor in his own country when the philological activity on the part of the English eighteenth-century scholars was taking place. Finally, in 1797–98, Juan Pellicer published an edition with footnotes, the forerunner of the great erudite editions of the nineteenth century by Clemencín, Cortejón, and Rodríguez Marín.

The importance of *Don Quixote* as a model for the English prose fiction of the eighteenth century is undeniable. Both social satire and psychological insights are to be found in Cervantes' pages. The English novel developed precisely along these two directions, often combining both, exploring the mind of a character in order to show in detail how society, and more specifically the social class to which the character belonged, could be understood—and satirized—through its reflection upon one individual.

Daniel Defoe was one of the first to succumb to *Don Quixote's* charm: he complained that the book was a source of delight and merriment but was too often superficially understood. Tobias Smollett, after translating it into English, imitated it in *The Adventures of Sir Launcelot Greaves* and *The Adventures of Roderick Random*. The influence of Cervantes is also visible in Laurence Sterne's *Tristam Shandy* (1760–1767) and even *A Sentimental Journey* (1768). It could be argued that between these two novels his art undergoes an evolution not dissimilar to the evolution between the first and the second part of *Don Quixote*. He acquires a perfect sureness of touch: The *Sentimental Journey* is much more concentrated than the tangled mass of narrative and reflection and digression which constitutes *Tristam Shandy*. Sterne is more cynical than Cervantes: the animality in human nature is almost an obsession with him. Henry Fielding was also clearly influenced by Cervantes' novel: In *Don Quixote in England* he offered a Molièresque adaptation; *The History of the Adventures of Joseph Andrews and of his friend Mr. Abraham Adams* (1742) turns around a chief character, Adams, who is a noble example of primitive goodness and childlike Christian altruism and resembles Don Quixote; *Tom Jones*, a novel in which dialogue is essential and reveals the nature of each character, also bears Cervantes' imprint. The English novel is born therefore in the eighteenth century under the influence of *Don Quixote*. This development is a logical one, since the age of Enlightenment was also an age of satire—and Cervantes offered an excellent example of satire in the genre of the novel.

It can be said that Cervantes' novel was greeted in the seventeenth century with a laugh, in the eighteenth with a smile, and in the nineteenth with a tear. It is to the credit of the German Romantics that they were the first to give a deeper and more comprehensive reading to Cervantes' works: they recognized *Don Quixote* as the prototype of the modern novel, and saw in its main characters a balanced and dramatic synthesis of the opposing tendencies and feelings that animate the human spirit. Friedrich von Schelling showed how Cervantes' characters have a universal appeal because they satirize and symbolize permanent traits of man's psychology; Cervantes' aim was therefore much larger than the mere satire of romances of chivalry; he hailed the novel as a perfect model for all modern fiction. For Schelling, Cervantes is the greatest genius of European civilization, a modern Homer, and his masterpiece reconciles the epic and the dramatic genres within the framework of modern artistic sensibility.

The famous critic Wilhelm von Schlegel also saw in *Don Quixote* the expression of a conflict, the eternal struggle between the poetic and the prosaic aspects of human existence. Goethe admired Cervantes' novel and thought its reading was essential in the formation of the literary taste of his time. He felt linked to Cervantes by close bonds of spiritual affinity. Writing to Friedrich von Schiller, in December, 1795, he pointed out that in the *Exemplary Novels* he had come upon "a veritable treasury of delights and teachings" and that he had been happily surprised to find that they were "composed according to the same principles which we employ . . . in the kind of writing in which we ourselves are engaged."[3] Ludwig Tieck also highly praised Cervantes' short stories: he compared them to the Italian short stories and thought them superior because of their honesty and ethical commitment, their simplicity, their powerful analytical exactness. Friedrich von Schlegel concluded that the *Exemplary Novels* "are as valuable as *Don Quixote*, though they are less famous."[4]

In Russia Cervantes was admired, almost revered, since the second half of the eighteenth century. Pushkin, who read Spanish, translated *The Gypsy Girl*—and was influenced by this work, one of the sources of his admired poem, "The Gypsies." Gogol travelled to Spain and was an avid reader of Cervantes: his favorite short story seems to have been *The Dogs' Colloquy*. Ivan Turgenev made an excellent translation of *Rinconete and Cortadillo* and wrote a perceptive essay on Don Quixote and Hamlet.

The success of the *Exemplary Novels* was also a constant factor among French readers. A French version was published, translated by D'Audiguier and Rosset, in 1615, only a few months after the Castilian edition. It sold so quickly that nine consecutive editions appeared in a short time. Many Frenchmen learned Spanish with the help of a grammar, Cervantes' Spanish original, and its French translation. In the eighteenth century there seem to have been more editions of the *Exemplary Novels* in France than in Spain itself.

The nineteenth century is the golden age of Cervantes' fame and influence. The Italians Vittorio Alfieri (who had read the novel three times in French and once in Spanish), Ugo Foscolo, and Alessandro Manzoni were lavish in their praise. For the French critic Sainte-Beuve, *Don Quixote* was a faithful mirror of human reality. The quixotic type survived in Dickens' *Pickwick Papers*, in Alphonse Daudet's comic saga, *Tartarin de Tarascon*, in the main character of Dostoevski's *The Idiot*. As Turgenev wrote in his essay, *Hamlet and Don Quixote*, "Don Quixote personifies above all the problem of faith, of faith in something eternal, immutable, of faith in a truth higher than the individual . . . . In contrast to Hamlet, whose ego is the center of the world, there is not a single trace of egoism in Don Quixote; he is all abnegation and sacrifice." Sancho's greatest merit is his absolute fidelity, a fidelity "rooted in the sublime quality that the masses possess, that of blindly embracing an honored and good cause."[5]

Flaubert was also affected by Cervantes' influence. According to Ortega y Gasset, he wrote in *Madame Bovary* a transfiguration of the Don Quixote myth, setting it in modern times—and changing the sex of the main character: it is literature that turns the head and the heart of Flaubert's heroine, the cheap literature of second-rate romantic novels, as the cheap literature of romances of chivalry had driven mad the Spanish *hidalgo*. In American letters, clear traces of Cervantes' influence can be found in the obsessive hero of Melville's *Moby Dick*, Captain Ahab (it is probable that Melville had read *Don Quixote* shortly before conceiving his novel) and also in the picaresque wanderings of Mark Twain's couple in *Huckleberry Finn*. Cervantes' influence is so pervasive because the dilemma faced by his hero is still often our modern dilemma. As Robert Alter puts it, "Cervantes' down-at-the-heels Spanish gentleman, living in the country with a servant and a niece, tries to create for himself a role from literature because, as a rusting, functionless appurtenance of an iron age, he is no one in particular, and he wants desperately to become someone. The same is true, in different times and places, of a whole line of heroes of novels—Julien Sorel, Rastignac, Emma Bovary, Dorothea Brooke, Raskolnikov, Kafka's K., Leopold Bloom—all, whether pathetically or boldly, in search of an identity through the playing of a role . . . . And among recent American novelists, writers as different as Saul Bellow, John Barth, Bernard Malamud, Walker Percy, have created protagonists who, unsure of who they are or what they can possibly become, try on roles like clothing."[6] It is fitting to end this chapter with the words of a great modern novelist, Thomas Mann: at the end of his essay, *Voyage with Don Quixote,* he enumerates the feelings that pervade him after reading Cervantes' novel and thinking about its hero's life and death: "Pain, love, pity, and boundless reverence."[7]

Notes and References

Preface

1. *The Adventures of Don Quixote*, tr. J. M. Cohen (Baltimore, 1963), p. 30. Hereafter referred to as Cohen.
2. *Cervantes. A Collection of Critical Essays.* Ed. by Lowry Nelson, Jr. (Englewood Cliffs, 1969), p. 1.

Chapter One

1. For an interesting account of the preparations and the frame of mind of Philip II and his counselors, see Garrett Mattingly, *The Armada* (Boston, 1959), Chapters XVII and following.

Chapter Two

1. *Three Exemplary Novels*, tr. Samuel Putnam (New York, 1950), p. 151.
2. *Ibid.*, p. 152.
3. In *Obras completas* (Madrid, 1949), p. 179.
4. *Cervantes*, by Richard L. Predmore (New York, 1973), p. 49.
5. *Cervantes: his Life, his Times, his Works. Created by the Editors of Arnoldo Mondadori* (New York, 1970), p. 25.
6. The date traditionally given for Cervantes's departure from Naples is 20 September 1575. Professor Juan Bautista Avalle-Arce, however, has corrected this date and proved that Cervantes must have departed early in September. See "La Captura de Cervantes," *Boletín de la Real Academia Española*, 1968, p. 237-80.
7. Quoted by Predmore, *op. cit.*, p. 138.
8. *Ibid.*
9. *Obras completas, ed. cit.*, p. 1529.
10. *Historia de la literatura española. Edición revisada* (New York, 1963), I. 288.
11. *The Spain of Fernando de Rojas. The Intellectual and Social Landscape of La Celestina* (Princeton, 1972) p. 20.

Chapter Three

1. *Obras completas,* p. 66.
2. *Ibid.,* p. 63.
3. *Ibid.,* p. 58.
4. *Ibid.,* p. 87.
5. *Ibid.,* p. 82.
6. *Ibid.,* p. 51.
7. *Ibid.,* p. 60.
8. *Ibid.*

Chapter Four

1. *Obras completas,* p. 180.
2. *Don Quixote,* tr. by S. Putnam (New York, 1949), p. 430. Hereafter referred to as Putnam.
3. *Ibid.*
4. *Obras completas,* p. 104. We follow here James Y. Gibson's *Journey to Parnassus* (London, 1883), p. 275.
5. Predmore, *op. cit.,* p. 110.
6. Preface to *The Deceitful Marriage* (New York, 1963), page xxviii.
7. "On the Interludes of Cervantes," in *Cervantes. A Collection of Critical Essays,* ed. by Lowry Nelson, Jr., (Englewood Cliffs, 1969), p. 152.
8. *Ibid.,* p. 154.
9. *Ibid.,* p. 157.

Chapter Five

1. Starkie, *op. cit.,* p. xxxv.
2. *Ibid.,* p. viii.
3. Putnam, p. 426-27.
4. Starkie, *op. cit.,* p. viii.
5. *Ibid.,* p. xxxiv.
6. *Ibid.*
7. *Cervantes. Three Exemplary Novels.* Ed. by Juan Bautista Avalle-Arce (New York, 1964), p. 17.
8. In *Historia de la literatura española,* by Juan Luis Alborg (Madrid, 1967), II, 100.
9. Starkie, p. xxiv.
10. *Ibid.,* xxv.
11. Alborg, *op. cit.,* p. 101.
12. *Ibid.,* p. 103.
13. Starkie, p. 118-19.
14. "Cervantes and the Picaresque Mode," in *Cervantes. A Collection*

. . . etc., ed. by Lowry Nelson, Jr., pp. 138-39.
15. *Obras completas*, p. 834.
16. *Ibid.*, p. 852.
17. Art. quoted, p. 151 of the Lowry anthology.
18. See *El modelo del Licenciado Vidriera* by S. Rivera Manescan (Valladolid, 1947).
19. Introduction to *Cervantes. Three Exemplary Novels*, p. 21.
20. *Ibid.*, p. 23.
21. *Ibid.*, pp. 26-27.

Chapter Six

1. *Obras completas*, p. 609. On the subject of the Spanish pastoral tradition, see J. B. Avalle-Arce, *La novela pastoril española* (Madrid, 1959).
2. *Obras completas*, p. 1528.
3. *Ibid.*, p. 1001.
4. *Ibid.*
5. *Cervantes creador de la novela corta española* (Madrid, 1956), I, 22-23.
6. "Sobre La Galatea de Cervantes" in *Homenaje a Cercantes* (Valencia, 1950), p. 85.
7. *Obras completas*, pp. 621-22.
8. *Ibid.*
9. *Semblanzas y estudios españoles* (Princeton, 1956), p. 200.
10. *Cervantes* (Madrid, 1917), pp. 44-45.

Chapter Seven

1. Putnam, p. 12.
2. *Ibid.*, p. 16.
3. *Ibid.*, p. 531.
4. *Ibid.*
5. *Ibid.*
6. *Ibid.*, p. 988.
7. "Cervantes," in Lowry Nelson Jr.'s *Cervantes*. . ., p. 16.
8. *Ibid.*, p. 17.
9. Both incidents are described by J. L. Alborg, *op. cit.*, p. 141.
10. See his "Un aspecto en la elaboración del Quijote," in *Mis páginas preferidas. Temas literarios* (Madrid, 1957), p. 228 ff.
11. *Ibid.*, p. 234, note.
12. Quoted by Alborg, *Historia* . . . p. 143.
13. *Guía del lector del Quijote* (Madrid, 1926) p. 76.
14. *Op. cit.*, p. 4 (Introduction).

15. Putnam, p. 162.
16. *Ibid.*, p. 164.
17. *Ibid.*
18. *Ibid.*
19. Art. quoted, p. 19.
20. Putnam, p. 118.
21. *Ibid.*, pp. 29-30.
22. "The Enchanted Dulcinea," in Lowry Nelson's *Cervantes* . . . p. 108.
23. Putnam, p. 173.
24. *Literature as a System* (Princeton, 1971), p. 152.
25. "Literature and Life in *Don Quixote*," in Lowry Nelson's *Cervantes* . ., p. 124.
26. *Ibid.*, art. quoted, pp. 138-39.
27. Alter, *Fielding and the Novel* (New York, 1969), p. 182.
28. See Otis H. Green's "*El Licenciado Vidriera*: Its Relation to the *Viaje del Parnaso* and the *Examen de Ingenios* of Huarte," in Alessandro S. Crisafulli, ed., *Linguistic and Literary Studies in Honor of Helmut A. Hatzfeld* (Washington, D.C., 1964), pp. 214-15.
29. Art. quoted, in Lowry Nelson's Anthology, p. 127.
30. "On the Significance of Don Quixote," in L. Nelson's Anthology, p. 90.
31. *Ibid.*, p. 91.
32. Putnam, p. 42.
33. *Historia* . . . I, 307.
34. *Ibid.*, p. 308.
35. Quoted by A. del Río, *ibid.*

Chapter Eight

1. Putnam, p. 509.
2. *Ibid.*
3. Forcione, *Cervantes' Christian Romance. A Study of "Persiles y Sigismunda"* (Princeton, 1972), p. 52 ff.
4. Quoted by Forcione, *op. cit.*, p. 16.
5. Forcione, *Cervantes, Aristotle and the "Persiles"* (Princeton, 1970), p. 3.
6. Quoted by Forcione, *ibid.*, p. 26.
7. *Ibid.*, p. 16.
8. *Ibid.*, p. 87.
9. *Poetics*, XXIII. Quoted by Forcione, *op cit.*, p. 93.
10. Putnam, p. 426.
11. *Ibid.*

12. *Ibid.*, p. 426.

13. *Ibid.*, p. 427.

14. *Ibid.*, pp. 427-28.

15. *Cervantes, Aristotle* . . . p. 169.

16. Stanley, *The Wanderings of Persiles and Sigismunda* (London, 1854), Preface, p. 11.

17. *Cervantes' Christian Romance*, p. 30 ff.

18. *Obras completas*, p. 1529.

19. *The Wanderings* . . . pp. 394-95.

20. Amezúa, *Cervantes creador de la novela corta española*, I, pp. 409-10.

21. See Forcione, *Cervantes' Christian Romance*, p. 3.

22. *Ibid.*, p. 4.

23. *Ibid.*, p. 5.

24. Jung, *Symbols of Transformation*, tr. R. F. C. Hull, (Princeton, 1967), I, 205, 2C8.

25. *Obras completas*, p. 1529.

Chapter Nine

1. *Obras completas*, p. 1523.

2. Thus in a letter to a friend in Valladolid. Lope also claimed there was "no poet so bad as Cervantes." For the complete text, see L. Astrana Marín, *Vida ejemplar y heroica de Miguel de Cervantes Saavedra* (Madrid, 1948), VI, 141-42.

3. Quoted in *Cervantes: His Life, His Times, His Works, Created by the Editors of Arnoldo Mondadori*, p. 155.

4. *Ibid.*

5. *Ibid.*, pp. 160-61.

6. Alter, *Fielding and the Novel*, p. 77.

7. "Voyage with Don Quixote," in *Cervantes* . . . ed. by Lowry Nelson, Jr., p. 72.

Selected Bibliography

PRIMARY SOURCES

The Spanish editions of Cervantes' works are innumerable. The text is usually the same, only the footnotes, introductions and illustrations vary. Two editions deserve special mention:

El ingenioso hidalgo Don Quijote de la Mancha. Edición y notas de Francisco Rodríguez Marín. (Madrid: Espasa-Calpe, S.A., 1935). The notes are abundant, scholarly.

Obras completas. Recopilación, estudio preliminar, prólogos y notas por Angel Valbuena Prat. (Madrid: Aguilar, 1949). A complete, compact, practical edition.

Two important translations of *Don Quixote* into English:

Don Quixote, A New Translation . . . by Samuel Putnam (New York: The Viking Press, 1949). Good literary translation.

The Adventures of Don Quixote. Tr. by J. M. Cohen (Baltimore: Penguin, 1963). Clear and modern language.

SECONDARY SOURCES

Again, short of writing a book, it is impossible to quote but a few:

AVALLE-ARCE, JUAN B. *Deslindes cervantinos* (Madrid: Edhigar, 1961). Intelligent essays on Cervantes' times and attitudes.

AVALLE-ARCE, J. B. and RILEY, E. C., eds. *Suma Cervantina.* London, Tamesis Books Limited 1973. An interesting collection of critical essays by the world's leading Cervantes specialists. The "last word" of scholarship on Cervantes' life and works.

CASTRO, AMÉRICO. *El pensamiento de Cervantes.* Nueva ed. (Madrid-Barcelona: Noguer, 1972). Solid essays on Cervantes' cultural background.

Hacia Cervantes. Nueva ed. (Madrid: Taurus, 1960). On Erasmus, the Inquisition, ideological conflict in Cervantes' time.

DURAN, MANUEL. *La ambigüedad en el Quijote* (Xalapa: Universidad veracruzana, 1960). On perspectivism and relativism in Cervantes.

ENTWISTLE, WILLIAM. *Cervantes* (Oxford: The Clarendon Press, 1940). Clear and well organized.

FLORES, ANGEL, and BENARDETE, M. J., eds. *Cervantes Across the Centuries* (New York: The Dryden Press, 1947). First-rate essays by Leo Spitzer, Américo Castro, and many other important scholars.

MADARIAGA, SALVADOR DE. *Don Quixote: An Introductory Essay in Psychology* (Oxford: The Clarendon Press, 1935). An intelligent, perceptive essay on the Don Quixote-Sancho relationship.

MENDEZ PEÑATE, SERGIO. *Estudio estilístico del Quijote* (Salamanca: Graficesa, 1972.) Clear, up to date.

NELSON, LOWRY, ed. *Cervantes. A Collection of Critical Essays.* (Englewood Cliffs: Prentice-Hall, 1969). An excellent authology with essays by Blanco Aguinaga, Harry Levin, Thomas Mann, Leo Spitzer, E. C. Riley, etc.

PREDMORE, RICHARD L. *Cervantes* (New York: Dodd, Mead & Co., 1973). An up-to-date biography, scholarly and easy to read. Many illustrations.

RILEY, E. C. *Cervantes' Theory of the Novel* (Oxford: The Clarendon Press, 1962). A perceptive analysis of Cervantes' ideas on literature and thee way they affected his writings.

Index